Understanding the Qur'an

Anton Wessels

scm press

Translated by John Bowden from the fourth edition of the Dutch *De Koran Verstaan, Een kennismaking met het boek van de islam,* published 2000 by Uitgeverij Kok, Kampen.

SCM Press wishes to express its deep gratitude to the Van Coeverden-Adriani Stichting for a grant towards the cost of translation, which made the publication of this book possible

0 334 02804 3

English translation first published 2000 by
SCM Press
9–17 St Albans Place, London N1 0NX

SCM Press is a division of
SCM-Canterbury Press Ltd

Typeset by Regent Typesetting, London
Printed in Great Britain by
Biddles Ltd, Guildford and King's Lynn

Contents

1

Introduction: The Opening Chapter of the Qur'an

'None but the purified shall touch it (the book)', 56.79 (78)

Qur'an literally means 'recitation', what has to be read out, recited. It is what the Prophet Muhammad receives as a revelation from God and has to recite to others.

The Qur'an is a book which is intended to be *heard* rather than *read*. It is recited by and for Muslims on all kinds of occasions from the cradle to the grave. Radio Cairo has a station that broadcasts Qur'anic texts twenty-four hours a day. The greatest care is taken with the recitation. Every year in the Islamic world there are competitions in reciting the Qur'an. From his youth, every Muslim boy learns certain passages from the Qur'an by heart, above all the first chapter and the last short chapters.

This book is meant to be a guide to reading and learning to read the Qur'an. It almost goes without saying that it cannot discuss the whole content of the Qur'an. Here I shall simply be looking at selected chapters. The book is meant to make the Qur'an rather more familiar to the English reader. I hope at least that those who have read these chapters and above all have done the exercises at the end of them – in other words who have really looked up the references to the Qur'an and read these passages – will be able to find their way around the Qur'an better. As the Qur'an says about the Torah, cf. 5.44 (48) and the Gospel, 5.46 (50), the Qur'an is meant to be a light, 42.52; cf. 31.20 (19), 35.25.

The Qur'an is not an easy book. It is more difficult to read than the Bible. The style is sometimes jerky, sometimes even staccato. Some sentences do not flow and are unfinished. Sometimes you ask yourself precisely what they are about, precisely what this or that refers to. Readers constantly need a commentary and elucidation to understand the drift of a passage.

Often the reaction of the reader who is familiar with the Bible will be that the stories in the Qur'an which are in one way or another the same as, or similar to, the Bible seem particularly fragmentary. Sometimes one even supposes that persons are confused and interchanged. In this connection I have noted the following. In the Qur'an Haman, who in the book of Esther is the servant of Ahasuerus, the king of the Medes and Persians, is said to be a servant of Pharaoh 28.6 (5). Along with Pharaoh and his armies he is said to be a sinner, 28.8 (7). He is mentioned in the same breath as Korah and Pharaoh, to whom Moses comes with proofs of his mission. But they are arrogant 29.39 (38). All three, Korah, Pharaoh and Haman, regard Moses as a 'lying magician', 40,24 (25).

Another example of such confusion is Mary the mother of Jesus, who seems to be identified with Miriam the sister of Moses and Aaron. In the Qur'an, Mary, the mother of Jesus, is said to be the sister of Aaron (Harun), 19.28 (29). In the Qur'an, Amram (Imram) is seen as the father of Mary (the mother of Jesus), 66.12; cf.3.33–37(30–32). In the Bible Amram is the father of Moses, Aaron and their sister Miriam, Numbers 26.59.

Probably it is too simplistic to speak here of confusion or substitution. It seems improbable that Muhammad thought that Jesus and Moses were cousins. Clearly the Qur'an makes connections which historically speaking do not 'fit' but which agree with its message. It is not a matter of giving information but of passing on a message. That the Qur'an is concerned to do something other than give an accurate historical description can also be illustrated both from particular stories which are also known from the Bible and from allusions to events at the time of Muhammad's life. In both cases often the names of persons and places are not given. This is true of stories about Eve 2.35 (33); Cain and Abel 5.30 (33); Sodom and Gomorrah 15.61–77; Potiphar and his wife, 12.21; Benjamin, 12.63–66; Nineveh, 10.98; Jerusalem ,17.1. Nor are the names mentioned of Abu Bakr, 9.30; Ayesha, 24.11–16; and Zaynab bint Jahsh en Zayd, 33.36, 37. The only woman whose name is given in the Qur'an is Mary!

Be this as it may, it is certain that Muhammad did not have a text of the Bible in his hand and that he can never have known it in this sense. In so far as he is informed about the Bible, it must have been by oral tradition. We shall probably never be able to determine how much or how little information he had. But the Qur'an will be read wrongly if one starts by asking whether or not a particular biblical story has been handed down complete or possibly even in a mutilated form. The real concern of the Qur'an can perhaps best be made clear from the following example. In the Qur'an there are references to events from the life of Muhammad and his community, as for example the battles of Badr and Uhud.

At this point the reporting in the Qur'an is fragmentary. In this case it is of course clear that there is no question that it is not well informed. So certainly the reference to such an event is aimed at something other than describing it. Even then, no event is described, but insight is given into an event, for example, that history takes place in accordance with the will of God. Therefore the style of the Qur'an can be said to be more evocative; it evokes something other than the description of something or someone. It is in the first place concerned to edify and teach. The content is more prescriptive than descriptive. The information does not come first. The Qur'an seeks to address the reader, involve the reader in what is being said. The Qur'an seeks to draw people from the errors of their ways, make the blind see, bring knowledge and create insight for the ignorant.

Translating the Qur'an

Reading the Qur'an is made more difficult by the fact that we usually depend on a translation. The Qur'an is written in Arabic. For a long time Muslims thought that this book could not, indeed must not, be translated. This notion is not so strange. In Latin there is an expression which puts the problem of translation well: *traductor traditor*, the translator is a traitor. Anyone who has tried to translate something from one language to another knows that really this never completely succeeds. There are those words and expressions which cannot be translated and expressed in another language with the same content and connotations. Muslims have felt this problem even more strongly in the translation of the Qur'an than Christians have in the translation of the Bible. Reformation Christians are familiar with the references by preachers in their sermons to the original text (Hebrew for the Old Testament and Greek for the New). Behind that is the justified feeling that despite the sometimes admirable translation it is necessary to refer back to the original text to understand a passage properly. That remains a condition for proper exegesis. For centuries Muslims did not want to translate the Qur'an, not only because they were afraid of 'betraying' the original text, but also because they were convinced that the beauty of this Arabic text, which indicates its divine origin, makes it impossible to translate.

The Qur'an tells us that Muhammad challenges his opponents, who do not believe that he brings a message from God, to produce something similar; cf. 2.23 (21); 10.38 (39); 11.13; 12.88 (90). The presupposition is of course that Muhammad's opponents must fail to meet this challenge. But in the long run even Muslims themselves began to translate the Qur'an into other languages. However, the fact that people prepare to call such a translation a commentary on or exposition of the Qur'an rather than the Qur'an itself shows that the starting point here really remains the same. For instance, the title of an English translation of the Qur'an by a Muslim is not *Qur'an* but *The Eternal Message of the Qur'an*, although we feel that it is a translation and not a commentary. Another classic English translation is entitled *The*

Qur'an Interpreted. This translation, by A.J.Arberry, is to my mind the most poetic English translation, so the quotations in this English edition of my book will be based on it. However, now and then slight adjustments have had to be made where a point needs to be brought out, or the transliteration is now outdated. (Since o and e are not Arabic vowels, it is more normal now, and more correct, to speak of the Qur'an rather than the Koran, and Muhammad rather than Mohammed.)

Division

The Qur'an is divided into 114 chapters or sections. Each section is called a *surah*. These chapters are in turn divided into verses, in Arabic *aya* in the singular and *ayat* in the plural. The Arabic word means both 'sign' and 'miracle'.

The Qur'an says of prophets before Muhammad that they performed miracles. Moses strikes a rock with a staff and thereupon twelve sources spring out, 2.60 (57). Jesus makes birds out of clay and breathes life into them, 5.110; 3.49 (34); he heals the blind and lepers, 3.49 (43); 5.110, raises the dead, 3.49 (43); 5.110; and asks God to make a table descend from heaven, 5.112–115. According to the Qur'an Muhammad does no miracles in this sense of the word. The only miracle that he produces is the Qur'an. All the verses, *ayat,* are wonders or signs of God.

Chapter 62, verse 2, or if one wants to say it in full, *surah* (= chapter) 'Congregation' (as well as a number, each chapter has a name, see Chapter 2 below), *aya* or verse 2, says:

> 'It is He (God) who has raised up from among the common people a Messenger from among them, to recite His verses (*ayat*) to them,' 62.2 (I shall regularly refer to the Qur'an in this form).

Muhammad is warned not to be deterred from these signs by unbelievers, 28.87.

The way in which the Qur'an is arranged is by length of chapter. The second chapter – the first is a brief opening prayer – is the longest . Each successive chapter is shorter. The shortest chapters come at the end of the Qur'an. Now historically speaking the longer parts will mostly be later, whereas the shortest usually come from the initial period of Muhammad's activity. So if we want to read the Qur'an in chronological order we do best to begin at the end. The early editions of Dawood's English translation in Penguin Books which put the Qur'an in this order are a good example of this approach, and this translation is quite useful as a first introduction to reading the Qur'an (in later editions, Dawood returned to the Qur'anic order).

You may note that in many of the translations of the Qur'an different numberings of the verses occur. This is because the division of the Arabic Cairo edition into verses differs from the current Western editions. Because this difference can cause problems, in this book both numbers are given if there is a difference between them. Moreover I have translated the name Allah by God. Where names appear both in the Bible and in the Qur'an, I use the biblical terminology.

In many translations of the Qur'an, above each chapter it is indicated whether this was revealed in Mecca or Medina. (Muhammad was active first in Mecca from around 610 to the emigration to Medina in 622, and afterwards in Medina from 622 to his death in 632.)

In the exegesis of the Qur'an Muslims themselves have paid a good deal of attention to the causes or occasions of the revelation (or descent). Scholars try to establish in what situation and circumstance the different Qur'an texts were revealed. It is clear that such a science is very important for understanding and expounding the different texts.

In study of the Qur'an in the West many investigations have been made in an attempt to establish the chronological order of the Qur'an texts. By means of the chronological order, people have tried to chart the development of the patterns of thought in the Qur'an. In this way three periods in Mecca and one in Medina are distinguished.

Recitation

Before you begin to read the Qur'an it is worth reflecting on what generally is the function of the Qur'an for Muslims. As I have said, it is really first of all a book that is recited, rather than read. First of all, note must be taken of the 'liturgical' function. How many Muslims could (and in some cases even now can) read and write? Here the situation is not very different from that of Christian believers with respect to the Bible in the Middle Ages. But after all, even then the Bible was known. During the liturgy, above all in the Orthodox churches, the Bible is solemnly brought in, as traditionally it always has been, and passages are read out of it. In a comparable way the Qur'an is recited on all kinds of occasions, as at the time of ritual prayer (*salat*) or during Ramadan, the month of fasting. Although no comparison really works, it is possible finally to understand the significance of the Qur'an for Christians by comparing it with the significance of Jesus for Christians. Just as for Christians Jesus is the word of God, 'the Word made flesh', John 1.14, so for Muslims the Qur'an is the word of the living God: 'the Word made book'.

A Muslim thinker makes the point like this:

> The word of God in Islam is the Qur'an; in Christianity it is Christ. The vehicle of divine revelation in Christianity is the Blessed Virgin; in Islam it is the soul of the Prophet. The Prophet must be illiterate

for the same reason that the Virgin Mary must be virgin. The human vehicle of a divine message must be pure and unconscious. The divine word can be written only on the clean and unwritten sheet of human receptivity. If this word is in the form of a book, then this purity is symbolized by the illiteracy of the person who is chosen to make this word known among people. Both (the illiteracy of the Prophet and the virginity of Mary) symbolize a deep aspect of this mystery of revelation.

Every recitation of the Qur'an begins with a formula in which refuge is sought with God from the accursed Satan (*al shaytan al-rajim*). The Qur'an itself invites this:

> 'When thou recitest the Qur'an, seek refuge in God from the accursed Satan,' 16.98 (100).

The Qur'an asserts that Muhammad is not someone who speaks the words of the accursed Satan, 81.25. God preserves people from any accursed Satan, 15.17; cf. 3.36 (31).

The word translated 'accursed' also means 'stone'. During the pilgrimage to Mecca (*haj*), in one of the rites Satan is stoned in order to indicate that people wholly turn away from Satan's tricks and wiles:

> 'And say, "O my Lord, I take refuge in Thee from the evil suggestions of the Satan,"' 23.97 (99).

The opening chapter

It is obvious that one begins reading the Qur'an from the beginning, at the opening chapter which also bears this name. It is a prayer which is prayed by Muslims on all kinds of occasions inside and outside the mosque, together and in private. So it roughly has the function of the 'Our Father' in the Christian tradition.

There is another reason for beginning with a look at the first chapter. The pious mystical tradition says that the whole Qur'an is summed up in this first chapter, the whole of the first chapter in the *bismillah* (in the name of God) and the whole *bismillah* in the point under the first Arabic letter *bab* (ب), the drop from the pen (*qalam*) with which God has taught, 96.4.

In other words, the thought is that the quintessence of Islamic teaching is contained in this chapter.

The translation runs:

> 'In the Name of God, the Merciful, the Compassionate.
> Praise belongs to God, the Lord of all Being,
> the All-merciful, the All-compassionate,
> the Master of the Day of Doom.

Thee only we serve; to Thee alone we pray for succour.
Guide us in the straight path,
the path of those whom Thou hast blessed,
not of those against whom Thou art wrathful,
nor of those who are astray,' 1.1–8 (1–7).

Like all the others – with the exception of the ninth, for some inexplicable reason – this chapter begins with the *bismillah al-rahman al-rahim*, 'In the Name of God, the Merciful, the Compassionate'. This invocation calls down God's blessing on an action. A pious Muslim uses it at the beginning of a journey, when getting up or going to sleep. It cannot lightly be left out of an book published by Muslims. Speeches and letters begin with it. This usage is inspired by the Qur'an itself, as is evident from the following examples. The Qur'an mentions the letter which Solomon sends to the Queen of Sheba. This begins with 'In the Name of God,' 27.30.

When Noah enters the ark, that likewise takes place in God's name:

'He (Noah) said, "Embark in it! In God's Name
shall be its course and its berthing,"' 11.41 (43).

The divine name *Rahman*, the Merciful, occurs many times in the Qur'an and seems to be an independent name. This name for God was known in South Arabia in the pre-Islamic period, as is evident among other things from an inscription which has been found there.

In preaching on the Qur'an this divine name emphasizes the absolute mercy of the only God. Whatever is said about the Merciful One in the Qur'an is said elsewhere about God.

It is striking that this divine name is used many times, above all in connection with the story about Jesus and Mary in the nineteenth chapter of the Qur'an, 19.18, 26, 44 (45), 45 (46), 58 (59), 61 (62), 69 (70), 75 (76), 78 (81), 85 (88), 87 (90), 88 (91), 91 (93), 93 (94), 96.

The combination of names, Merciful and Compassionate, also occurs elsewhere, 41.2; 2.163 (158); 59.22.

Al-Hamdullillah, 'Praise belongs to God', is an expression often used in the everyday Muslim Arabic vocabulary. The expression similarly occurs in the following verses: 6.45; 10.10 (11); 37.182; 39.75; 40.65; also 45.36 (35); 7.54 (52); 40.64 (66); 27.8.

The expression 'Praise belongs to the Lord' also occurs at the beginning of a number of the chapters, 6, 8, 34, 35.

'Lord of all Being': *'Alamin* is an Aramaic loan word which means 'worlds'. However, it is used in the Qur'an in particular to denote the *inhabitants* of the world. In a great many passages in the Qur'an it means something like people: 6.90; 12.104; 38.87; 68.52; 81.27; 25.3; 29.10 (9); 26.165; 15.70.

The prayer for right guidance recalls Psalm 139. The Qur'an evokes more associations with the psalms, for example the parallel between Psalm 1 and this first chapter; cf. also Ps.27.11. The right way is often understood to mean Islam. According to the later Muslim commentators, the formulae 'those about whom God is wrathful' refers to the Jews and 'those who are astray' to the Christians. Because this is an early Meccan chapter, however, this interpretation is by no means obvious.

Presumably originally other groups of opponents – polytheists – in Mecca were meant.

Similar expressions, 'with whom He is wroth', 5.60 (65), and 'who have gone astray', 5.77 (81), elsewhere denote opponents in Medina. But 58.14 (15) is about dealing with the hypocrites who make common cause with the Jews.

'Hast thou not regarded those who have taken for friends a people *against whom God is wrathful*?'; cf. also 60.13.

A programme

After this 'opening prayer' the first verses of the second chapter sound like a programme. It is made clear in a nutshell what may be expected next:

> 'That is the Book, wherein is no doubt, a guidance to the godfearing who believe in the Unseen, and perform the prayer (*salat*), and expend of that We have provided them; who believe in what has been sent down to thee, and what has been sent down before thee, and have faith in the Hereafter,' 2.2–4 (2–3).

Variations on what later will be called the five pillars of Islam like *salat* and *zakat* really already appear here. The Qur'an presents itself as 'guidance to the people', 2.185.

The focal point is really human beings and their behaviour before the face of God.

Passages to look up

Anyone who really wants to learn to read the Qur'an should also look up all the references given in this book where the complete translation of the text is not given.

With the help of the index it is possible to look up and read a few narratives in which one is primarily interested.

It is clear how often events in the Bible and also events from the life of Muhammad and his community are simply alluded to rather than being related at length if one looks up in the Qur'an, with the help of the index, some of the stories from the Bible (e.g. about David) or from the life of Muhammad (for example about the battle of Badr).

2

A Survey of the Content of the Qur'an

'Say: "If the sea were ink for the Words of my Lord, the sea would be spent before the Words of my Lord are spent, though We brought replenishment the like of it,"' 18.109.

Introduction

I shall now give a survey of the various chapters of the Qur'an. In each case I shall explain the meaning of the title. Usually it is taken from a passage from the chapter concerned. In this way the content of the *surah* is given as briefly as possible; just a number of the most important subjects are indicated.

One way in which you can to some degree define the chronological order of the different chapters is by noting elements which are characteristic, for example, of the earliest revelations. Thus the oldest parts of the Qur'an are characterized by a rhyming prose; unfortunately this cannot be rendered well in most translations; cf. 90; 96.

An obvious characteristic of the earliest revelations is the appearance of oath formulae, a genre which was also customary among soothsayers (*kahin*) in the time of Muhammad. Thus certain 'things' are sworn which are connected in one case with angels, in another with winds and sometimes with war horses, 51.1–4; 77.1–7; 79.1–5; 100.1–5; 37.1–3. Oaths are also sworn by the morning light, the dawn, the noon, the night, heaven, the moon, the stars, 93.1, 2; 103, 1; 84.16–18; 74.32–34 (35–37); 92.1, 2; 89.1–4; 53.1; 86. 1; 85.1; 81.15–18; 56.75 (74); 86.11, 12.

These oath formulae do not appear at a later stage. Then there are oaths by the 'day of resurrection', 43.1; 44.1 or by 'the Qur'an', 50.1; 38.1; 36.1. Later even that is no longer done and formulae appear like:

> 'Those are the signs of the Book and of a manifest Qur'an,' 15.1.

Here is an example of one of the stereotyped expressions in the Qur'an. When the unbelievers, hypocrites or polytheists say something, Muhammad then has to say something back in the name of God. The words of the former are introduced by 'they (the unbelievers) say', and Muhammad's words in the name of God are introduced by the expression 'Say', cf. 22.71 (71); 23.84–89 (86–91).

The preaching of the Qur'an is initially addressed to the Meccans;

later it is also addressed to the inhabitants of Medina and finally to the Bedouins in Arabia. The context, which becomes increasingly wide, also comes out in a beginning like 'O men'.

Twenty-four chapters of the Qur'an are called Medinan. Often editions of the Qur'an indicate whether the chapters are Meccan or Medinan.

Titles and short descriptions of all 114 chapters

1. The Opening
The first chapter is called 'opening chapter'.
It is used as a prayer and functions rather like the 'Lord's Prayer' in the Christian tradition (cf. the Introduction).

2. The Cow
This name is taken from v.67, which states that Moses said to his people that God had ordered them to slaughter a cow. A connection has been seen with Numbers 19.1–9 and Deuteronomy 21.1–9. This longest chapter of the Qur'an goes into the relationship between the Muslim community and the Jews and Judaism. Among other things it dwells on the fall of Adam, 30–39 (28–37). In the extended passage about the relationship to the Jews, 40–121 (38–115), the Qur'an refers to Abraham, who is seen as a kind of founder of Islam and who erected the Ka'ba, 121–141 (118–135). The change in the direction of prayer from Jerusalem to Mecca is also discussed, 142–152 (136–147).

A good deal of the chapter is then devoted to regulations for the young Muslim community, 153–243 (148–244).

3. The House of Imram (Amram)
Verse 33 (39) says that God chose the generation of Imram above all men, after that of Adam, Noah and Abraham. In the Bible Imram is called the father of Moses, Exodus 6.19. In 3.35 (31) he is presented as the father of Mary.

Many of the events described here are connected with the battle of Uhud in March 625 (for a survey of the events in Muhammad's life see Appendix 2).

In this chapter there is also a passage about Jesus, 42–64 (37–57); cf. *surah* 19.

4. Women
The title is taken from the third verse, which is about the possibility of being married to at most four women at the same time. It contains all kinds of passages in connection with the law of inheritance, 7–14

(8–18); there are passages directed against the Jews, 44–57 (47–60) and the hypocrites, 138–149 (147–148); what is regarded as the Christian doctrine of the Trinity is disputed, 171–173 (169–173). In fact, however, this passage is about tritheism.

5. The Table

The title is taken from v.112, where the disciples of Jesus ask him to request his Lord to make a table descend from heaven. The story in some ways resembles Peter's vision in Acts 10. The Arabic word for table used here is an Ethiopian loan word, where it means 'table of the Lord'.

The first verses are about food laws, 1–5 (1–7); there are attacks on Jews and Christians, 2–26 (15–29) and passages directed only against the Jews (including the story of Cain and Abel), 27–45, and again a passage directed against both Jews and Christians 51–86 (56–88). In the following part there are again food laws, 87,88 (89,90).

6. Cattle

For the title cf. v.136 (137). This chapter is about a variety of subjects including Abraham and his descendants, 74–90; about unbelieving Meccans, 25–32, 109–127; and about the signs of God, 95–99.

7. The Battlements

The title is taken from v. 46 (44), which speaks of a partition between heaven and the inhabitants of hell. On the walls stand men who know believers and unbelievers by their signs; cf. 57.13. This chapter contains the creation story 10–35 (9–33), some stories of prophets like Noah, Hud, Salih, Lot, Sju'ayb, 59–102 (57–200), and the history of Moses and the Israelites, 103–169 (101–168).

8. The Spoils

The title is taken from the first verse, which is about the question of the spoils which were taken in the battle of Badr.

A good deal of the chapter is about the dispute between the unbelievers in the period between Badr and the battle of Uhud.

9. Repentance

The title is taken from v.3, which speaks about the importance of repentance. This chapter, which comes from the last period of Muhammad's activity, contains all kinds of subjects connected with war and battles in 631. The first 36 verses contain the proclamation by Muhammad that he possibly had his cousin and son-in-law Ali read out during the pilgrimage in 630.

This is the only chapter which begins without the usual introductory words, 'In the name of God, the Compassionate, the Merciful'. It is sometimes thought that this chapter and the previous one belong together.

Muhammad is said to have said that he was anxious about this and the eleventh chapter.

10. Jonah

This is the first example of a chapter which bears the name of a prophet. In v.98 Jonah is mentioned for the first time. Like the seventh chapter, this contains a description of earlier messengers: Noah, 71–73 (72–74); Moses and Aaron, 75–93 (76–93); and of course Jonah, 98–100.

11. Hud

Hud is the name of a so-called Arab prophet like Sju'ayb and Salih, who unlike the other prophets is not mentioned in the Bible. The name is taken from v.50.

A good deal of this chapter discusses the history of the Arab and other prophets: Noah, 25–49 (27–51); Hud, who is sent to the people of 'Ad, 50–60 (52–63); Salih, who is sent to Thamud, 61–68 (64–71); Abraham, 69–76 (72–78); Lot, 77–83 (79–84); Sju'ayb, who is sent to Midian, 84–95 (85–98); and Moses, 96–99 (99–101).

12. Joseph

This whole chapter is about Joseph. The name appears for the first time in the fourth verse.

The last part, 102–111 (103–111), draws a kind of conclusion or lesson from the story of Joseph.

13. Thunder

Like the second and the following two chapters, this begins with 'mysterious' letters. 'God alone knows the meaning.' In the thirteenth verse it is said that the thunder praises God. This might remind us of Psalm 29.

The chapter consists of short units, some of which deal with the task of God's messenger – to hand on what is revealed to him – and what happens to him in the process, 30–32 (29–23), 40–43.

14. Abraham

The name of this chapter is taken from the famous patriarch. He is mentioned for the first time in v.35 (38).

This chapter also speaks of Abraham, 35–40 (38–42); Moses, 4–7; and former messengers who have been sent to the people of Noah, Hud and Salih, 9–14 (9–17).

15. Hijr

The name Hijr, that of a city in the north of the Hejaz which no longer exists, is taken from v.80, which speaks about the people of Hijr. These people are identified with the people of Thamud to whom Salih is sent as a messenger, cf. 7.75–79 (73–77); 11.61–68 (64–71).

Among other things this chapter discusses Satan (Iblis) and the creation of human beings, 28–42; the guests who visited Abraham, 49–60; and Lot and the overthrow of Sodom and Gomorrah, 61–77.

16. The Bee

This title is taken from v.68 (70), which says that God inspired the bees to make their homes in the mountains. It is the only time in the Qur'an that bees are mentioned. This chapter also speaks about God's creation, 3–16, and how unbelievers and believers respectively react to revelation, 24–29 (26–31), 30–32 (32–34).

17. The Night Journey

This title, which occurs in the first verse, refers to the night (mystical) journey which Muhammad is said to have made from the consecrated house in Mecca to the most distant house of prayer in Jerusalem.

Part of this chapter is directed against the Jews, 2–8. Verses 22–52 (23–54) contain all kinds of regulations for believers. Verse 88 (90) says that the Qur'an cannot be imitated.

18. The Cave

This chapter takes its title – v. 9 (8) – from the narrative of the young men who did not know how long they had stayed in a cave. This is an illusion to the story of the seven sleepers of Ephesus about whom there is a Christian legend.

They are said to have sought refuge in a cave during a persecution under Emperor Decius (249–251) and to have slept there for many years. In the Qur'an it is often said that on the day of resurrection the sinners think that the time they spent in the world before this resurrection lasted only for a brief span, 2.249 (250); 17.52 (54); 20.104; 23.112–114 (114–116).

This chapter also contains a parable about various owners of a vineyard, 32–44 (31–42); it is also about Moses, 60–82 (59–81) and the servant of God not mentioned by name, who is later called the 'green man'), and about the history of Alexander the Great, 83–98.

19. Mary

This chapter mentions among other things the stories of Zechariah, 2–11 (2–12); John the Baptist, 12–15 (13–15); Mary and Jesus, 14–40

(16–41); and the stories of Abraham 41–50 (42–51) and some other prophets.

20. *Ta Ha*

This combination of letters occurs only here. There has been no satisfactory explanation of the meaning of this and similar combinations of letters.

Among other things the chapter deals with the story of Moses, 9–76 (8–78); the journey through the Red Sea, 77–78 (79–81); and the worship of the golden calf, 83–98 (85–98).

'Umar, later to become the second caliph, is said to have been converted by hearing v.14 recited, but cf. also *surah* 73.

21. *The Prophets*

The title is taken from the passages which deal with the prophets, like Moses, 47–70 (49–70); Abraham and Lot, 71–75; Noah, 76, 77; and also with David and Solomon, 78–82; and Job, 83–88.

22. *The Pilgrimage*

Pilgrimage, which is spoken of in v.27 (28), has become one of the five pillars of Islam. It was already practised in the period before Islam and was as it were islamicized by Muhammad.

Part of this chapter is about the Ka'ba and its erection by Abraham and Ishmael, 25–33 (25–34).

23. *The Believers*

The word 'believers' is used directly in the very first verse. The Qur'an draws a distinction between a believer and a Muslim, namely between the one who is outwardly a Muslim but without real belief and a Muslim who is also at the same time a believer.

This chapter contains brief mentions of the histories of Noah, 23–30 (22–31); the prophets after him, 31–44 (32–46); Moses and Mary and Jesus, 45–50 (47–52).

24. *Light*

The title is taken from the so-called 'light verse', v.35, which has become famous; it plays an important role in the mystical tradition of Islam.

Most of this chapter is taken up with the matter of the slander against Muhammad's wife Ayesha. During an expedition she had lost a necklace. She came back a day later than Muhammad in the company of a young man. The slander which was then uttered is refuted by the Qur'an, 11–20.

25. Salvation

The word 'salvation' appears in the first verse and is a term for 'revelation'. It can also mean something like deliverance or liberation. In most of the verses in which it occurs it is spoken of as 'given' or 'sent down', 'revealed' by a book; cf. 2.53 (59); 2.185 (181); 3.1(3); 8,29, 41 (42); 25.1.

There is also mention, among other things, of the signs of God's power in nature, 45–54 (47–56) and the characteristics of the true believer, 63–77.

26. The Poets

This title is taken from v.224, where the poets are mentioned only at the end. This is about those who are seen as opponents of the Prophet Muhammad. The poet is regarded as someone who is inspired by the *jinns*. In Muhammad's time poets fulfilled a kind of journalistic function and influenced public opinion. Apart from an individual whom Muhammad defended, most of them were opponents of Muhammad. Muhammad was opposed to being regarded as a poet; cf. 21.5; 26.224.

This chapter contains a number of stories about prophets: Moses, 10–68 (9–69); Abraham, 69–104; Noah, 105–22; Hud, 123–140; Salih, 141–159; and Lot, 160–191. Finally there is an important passage about the Arabic revelation imparted to Muhammad, 192–220.

27. The Ant

The ants are mentioned in v.18.

Among other things, the chapter is about Solomon and the Queen of Sheba, 15–44 (14–45); Salih, 45–53 (46–54); and Lot, 54–58 (55–59).

28. The Story

In this chapter – for story cf. v.25 – the story of Moses is told, 3–42 (2–42). Among other things it also contains the story of Korah, 26–82; cf. Numbers 16.

29. The Spider

Verse 41 (40) speaks of the parable of the spider whose house is weak; so are those who seek friends apart from God. Apart from this parable of the spider, 41–44 (40–43), brief mentions are made of Noah, 14, 15; Abraham, 16–27 (15–26); and Lot, 28–35 (27–34).

30. The Greeks

The title – in Arabic *Rum* – refers to the Greek civilization of Byzantium or the Byzantines. On the one hand there is an allusion to the victory which the Persians gained over the Greeks, and to the conquest of Jerusalem, and on the other to the prediction of the coming conquest of the Persians by the Greeks (under Emperor Heraclius). It is one of the few examples in the Qur'an of the occurrence of references to contemporary events outside Arabia.

31. Lokman

This Lokman mentioned in v.12 is an Arab hero who was granted a long life, 12–19 (11–18). He is already mentioned by pre-Islamic poets.

32. Prostration

Prostration is one of the postures in offering ritual prayer, *salat*, cf. v.15. Among other things there is mention of God the Creator, 4–9 (3–8), the day of the resurrection, 10–14 (9–14), and believers and unbelievers (15–22).

33. The Confederates

Verse 20 speaks about groups of unbelieving Meccans and Jews at the time of the trench warfare between Muhammad and his opponents in April 627, 9–24 (cf. Appendix 2)

This chapter also contains various passages about incidents with Muhammad's wives, for example the wife of his adopted son Zayd, called Zaynab, 4–8, 37–40. Various other verses are about Muhammad's wives, 28–40, 50–59.

34. Sheba

The inhabitants of Sheba are mentioned in v.15 (14). This chapter contains an allusion, 16 (15), to the breach of the Marib dam. This breach, which must have taken placed in the middle of the sixth century, led to the collapse of the irrigation system in Yemen. The chapter is also about David and Solomon, 10–14 (10–13) and the judgment that will befall the powerful and rich, 31–39 (30–38).

35. The Angels

In this chapter God is praised as 'creator'. Among other things it is also about the reward that believers and unbelievers may expect, 29–45 (26–45).

36. Ya Sin

Another example or a chapter which begins with cryptic letters.

It contains a section that deals with the fate that awaits believers and unbelievers, 45–68.

It is a popular chapter which is often quoted in connection with the dying and the dead, 77–83.

37. The Rangers
Presumably the title refers to angels who stand in rows, v.1; cf. 89.22 (23); 24.41.

This chapter also contains stories of prophets: Noah, 75–82 (72–80); Abraham, 83–113 (81–113); Moses and Aaron, 114–122; Elijah, 123–132; Lot, 133–138; and Jonah, 139–148.

38. Sad
Sad is a letter of the Arabic alphabet, v.1.

The chapter is also about Solomon, 29–40 (28–39); Job, 41–44 (40–44); and about the rebellion of Iblis, 71–84 (71–85).

39. The Companies
Verse 71 speaks about hordes of unbelievers who are driven to hell; it is a part that is about the last judgment, 67–75.

40. The Believers
Another title is 'forgiver'. In v. 3 (2) 'forgiver' appears as one of the names of God.

This chapter contains the story of Moses and Pharaoh, 23–50 (24–53).

41. Revelations well expounded
This title – v.3 (2) – refers to the verses of scripture which are clearly expounded as an Arabic Qur'an for those who have knowledge. This chapter talks among other things about the punishment that unbelievers (of 'Ad and Thamud) incur and the fate that unbelievers and believers can expect, 10–36 (18–30).

42. Counsel
Verse 38 (36) speaks of the mutual counselling of believers which determines their behaviour. It is a text which is often cited in modern times to illustrate how the Qur'an would stand for a democratic mode of government by the practise of mutual deliberation. There is something in it about the way in which the revelation is handed down, 51–52 (50–52).

43. Ornaments
The title refers to ornaments or jewellery which God would have been able to bring to the houses of the unbelievers, v.35 (34).

Among other things this chapter contains a passage about Abraham, 26–28 (25–27); Moses, 46–56 (45–56); and Jesus, 57–65.

44. Smoke
This chapter takes its title from v.10, which speaks of the smoke which will come from heaven on the last day.
The story of Pharaoh occurs in it, 17–33 (16–32).

45. Hobbling
Verse 28 (27) speaks of every community which awaits the judgment 'hobbling on their knees'; a whole passage, 27–37 (26–36), deals with this.

46. The Sand-Dunes
Verse 21 (20) speaks of the brother of 'Ad (a people to which the prophet Hud is sent), who brought a warning to his people in the dunes. This last is probably a place name. There is also discussion of attitude towards parents, 15–17 (14–17) and the *jinns* who are said to have been converted in Nakhla by the preaching of Muhammad after his return from Ta'if in 619 or 620; cf. *surah* 72.

47. Muhammad
The name of the Prophet Muhammad occurs in the second verse. Among other things there is a discussion of the resistance to faith and the resistance to striving and the lapse into unbelief, 16–38 (18–40).

48. Victory
The first verse speaks about success. 'Success' refers to the treaty of Hudaybiyya that Muhammad made with the Meccans. This treaty formed the first step on the way to the conquest of Mecca. Therefore this title is also thought to refer to the conquest of Mecca itself in 630.
Victory (*fath*), which literally means 'opening' – compare the first chapter of the Qur'an – is applied in the Qur'an to the victory at Badr, 8.19 or to the conquest of Mecca, 57.10.
Later *fath* becomes the technical term not only for the conquest of Mecca but for all the Muslim conquests: the opening up of a country to Islam. Among other things this chapter discusses the behaviour of the Arabians in the sense of Bedouins, 11–17.

49. Apartments
Verse 4 speaks of the apartments of Muhammad's wives. The Arabians (Bedouins) are addressed here, 14–18.

50. Qaf
Qaf is the opening letter of the chapter.
Here we find the longest discussion in the Qur'an of the resurrection of human beings, 15–37 (15–36).

51. *The Scatterers*

'By the swift scatterers' is the formulation of the oath with which this chapter opens.

The first verses are reminiscent of chapters 77, 79 and also 100. This chapter discusses Abraham (Lot and Sodom) and his guests, 24–37, and also Moses, 38–40.

52. *The Mount*

The mountain mentioned here is probably Sinai. The term appears in the framework of the formulation of an oath, 1. The scripture which is then mentioned may well be the Torah of Moses. This chapter talks of the last judgment and the reward in paradise, 9–28. There are also a series of warnings against unbelievers and the reaction which Muhammad must give to them, 29–44.

53. *The Star*

This saying stands in the formulation of an oath at the beginning. If elsewhere in the Qur'an we have revelations which Muhammad receives in words, here there is mention of visions which he has seen, 1–18; cf. 81.23; 17.1; 17.60 (62); 48. 27; 8.45.

In this chapter there are allusions to the pagan goddesses Al-Lat, Al-'Uzza and Manat, 19–30 (19–31).

54. *The Moon*

The first verse speaks about the splitting of the moon as a sign of the last day. Popular tradition relates the miracle that Muhammad is said to have performed by splitting the moon. The Qur'an itself does not speak about miracles which Muhammad is said to have done, except for his one miracle or 'sign', namely the Qur'an.

Noah, 9–17; the people of 'Ad; and the people of Thamud, 23–32; Lot, 33–40; and Pharaoh, 41,42 are mentioned in this chapter.

55. *The All-Merciful*

The All-Merciful is one of the names of God in the Qur'an.

The recurrent refrain is: 'Which of your Lord's blessings would you deny?'

56. *The Terror*

The title refers to the catastrophe of the judgment that is dawning and that marks the day of judgment, v.1. This chapter contains descriptions of the last judgment, 1–1; paradise, 11–40 (11–39); hell, 41–57 (40–57); and the elect and the damned, 83–96.

57. Iron
God has sent down iron, v.2, which when used for weapons has strength in it.

Because of the words with which they begin, chapters 57, 59, 61, 62, 64 are called the 'songs of praise'. But cf. also 87. This chapter contains an invocation to praise and the giving of contributions to the needy which is bound up with this. More is said about believers, hypocrites and unbelievers in 7.24.

58. The Disputer
'The Disputer' refers to a woman – v.3 – who came to Muhammad to complain about being in her view wrongly cast out.

59. The Mustering
This title 'mustering', 2, refers to the unbelieving Jews of a Jewish tribe from Medina, the Banu Nadir, who have been driven out of their dwellings.

60. The Woman Tested
Verse 10 speaks of putting women to the test to see if they really believe. This is about the relationship between believers and unbelievers, 1–9, and the association with women, believing or unbelieving, according to the treaty of Hudaybiyya, 10–13.

61. The Ranks
In v. 4 it is said that God loves the believers who fight in battle order on his way and stand as firm as a wall.

This chapter contains a text, v.6, which is interpreted as a prediction by Jesus of the coming of Muhammad. The last verse, 14, is also about Jesus.

62. Congregation
The title refers to the meeting of believers for Friday noon prayer.

The Arabic name for Friday is 'day of congregation'.

63. The Hypocrites
'Hypocrites' – v.3 – is the name of the followers of Muhammad who follow him in a hypocritical way. In the long run it becomes the designation for a particular political group.

64. Mutual Fraud
The title, taken from the ninth verse, is used for the 'fraud' which is practised on the day of judgment.

65. Divorce
This title refers to the negotiations – v.1 – over the conditions for divorce.

66. The Forbidding
In the first verses of this chapter God asks Muhammad why he has forbidden what God has allowed. This refers to an incident in which Muhammad had kept away from one of his wives because of intrigues among them.

67. The Kingdom
The first verse speaks of God's sovereignty over the whole world, and also about God as creator, 1–5; the reward which awaits unbelievers and believers, 6–12; and God's power and sustaining of creation, 13–30.

68. The Pen
The chapter begins with an oath by the pen. Presumably that is to be seen as a reference to earlier books. But it could equally refer to the deeds of men which are written down.

Muhammad is called on to be patient; here there is a reference to the example of Jonah, 48–50.

69. The Indubitable
The title, 1, refers to the punishment for misdeeds which certainly will come. This chapter is about the terrors of the last judgment, 13–18, the judgment that awaits good and bad in which they get their books in their right or left hands respectively, 19–37. The last passage makes it clear that Muhammad is neither a poet nor a soothsayer, but brings a true message, 38–52.

70. The Stairways
'The stairways' refers to the heavenly ladder up which the angels and the spirit ascend, 3,4. The chapter is about the last judgment, 1–8, and about what characterizes believers, 22–35, and unbelievers, 36–44.

71. Noah
This chapter is about Noah, although it expresses the experience of Muhammad himself.

72. The Jinns
The chapter begins with the story of the *jinns* who listened to Muhammad's message. On the return from Ta'if in 621 it is related that

a number of *jinns* were converted under the influence of Muhammad's preaching; cf. *surah* 46.

73. Enwrapped

The title refers to Muhammad who wrapped himself in a mantle, 1.

According to the tradition – cf. v.9 – this chapter becomes the occasion for 'Umar to convert.

(However, 20.14 is also mentioned in the same connection.)

The last verse, 20, contains a regulation for night prayer.

74. Shrouded

It is said of Muhammad that at the first revelation that he received he shrouded himself in his cloak.

The first seven verse are regarded as among the oldest verses of the Qur'an, if not the oldest.

Verses 43–46 (44–47) describe what has brought evildoers to hell.

75. The Resurrection

The first and sixth verses speak about the day of resurrection. It is said that God has raised the dead, 1–6, 36–40. The chapter is also about the recitation of the Qur'an by Muhammad, 16–19.

76. Man

The first verse mentions man. Verses 5–22 contain a description of what the pious are to expect in the future life.

77. The Loosed Ones

An oath is sworn by the angels or the winds that are loosed. This chapter is about the certainty and the error of the last judgment, with ever more frequent repetition of 'Woe to those who declare the judgment to be a lie.'

78. The Tiding

The unbelieving Meccans – v.2 – ask themselves what is being proclaimed by their fellow townsman Muhammad. An important part of this chapter is taken up with the proclamation of the judgment and the determination of the arrogant and those who fear God, 17–40 (17–41).

79. The Pluckers

This title stands in the formulation of an oath and possibly refers to angels who snatch souls. It is also about the last judgment, 6–14, 34–46, and about Moses and Pharaoh, 15–26.

80. He Frowned
Once when a blind man came to ask Muhammad for advice, Muhammad frowned. He then turned his back on the blind man in favour of someone who in his view was more important, a Qurayshi who he hoped would convert.

81. The Darkening
This title refers to the darkening of the sun, v.1, one of the phenomena at the dawning of the day of judgment.

Verses 8, 9 speak of those buried alive who are asked in the last judgment for what offence they were killed. Verses 15–29 are about Muhammad's reception of revelation.

82. The Splitting
In the last judgment heaven will split, 1. The chapter is about the day of judgment, above all vv.10–29.

83. The Stinters
'Woe to you' is spoken over those who stint and who tamper with weights.

84. The Rending
The first verse speaks of the rending of heaven. The chapter is about the last judgment, the signs which precede it and the fate that awaits believers and unbelievers.

85. The Constellations
The constellations are mentioned in the formulation of the oath with which the chapter opens. The people of the trench, 3, who are also mentioned, are connected with the burning of Christians of Najran (Yemen) in 523 by the Jewish king Dhu Nuwas. There may also be a thought of the young men in the fiery furnace, Daniel 3.

86. The Night-Star
An oath is sworn by heaven and the star which appears in the night. The God who creates also has the power to recreate.

87. The Most High
The name of God the Most High is praised in the first verse.

88. The Enveloper
This title – v.1 – refers to the overwhelming day on which man will be judged. Here among other things there is a description of hell and paradise, 1–16.

89. The Dawn

This is one of the first revelations. Among other things it discusses former peoples who have been punished, 6–14 (5–13).

90. The Land, or The Place

The oath is sworn by the place, in other words Mecca and its surroundings. The 'steep' way (which suggests something like the 'narrow' way as opposed to the 'broad' way, cf. Matthew 7.13, 14) is described, 10–20; cf. 89.17–20 (18–21).

91. The Sun

In this chapter there is an oath by the sun, and a contrast between sun and moon, day and night, heaven and earth. This chapter contains the first allusion (chronologically speaking) to Thamud in the Qur'an.

92. The Night

In the formulation of the oath, as in the previous chapter, there is a contrast between day and night. The fate that awaits believers and unbelievers, bliss and fire respectively, is described.

93. The Forenoon

Morning light, the part of the morning between dawn and midday, when the sun has become hot, is mentioned in the first verse. This chapter contains encouragement for the Prophet Muhammad.

94. The Expanding

This title refers to the expanding of Muhammad's breast, namely the encouragement which God has given Muhammad.

95. The Fig

The oath is sworn by the fig tree or olive tree.

96. The Blood-Clot

There is a reference in v.2 to a blood-clot. The Qur'an speaks on various occasions of the process of the growth from a blood-clot to the adult man.

This chapter is regarded as the first revelation. The first word, *iqra*, 'recite', has the same root as the word *qur'an*, namely what is to be recited.

97. Power

The revelation is sent down to Muhammad in the Night of Power. It is said to have been one of the last nights of the month of Ramadan, which for this reason is regarded as being very holy.

98. The Clear Sign
Both the Qur'an and the Prophet – v.2 – are seen as 'proofs'.

99. The Earthquake
The earth quakes in preparation for the last judgment.

100. The Chargers
This title is said to refer to charging horses or camels.

101. The Clattering
'The clattering', 'striking', or 'knocking at the door' refers to a description of the last judgment; cf. 69.4.

102. Rivalry
The title is taken from the first verse and refers to the pressure of those who constantly want to increase their possessions, 1.

103. Afternoon
An oath is sworn by the afternoon, 1.

104. The Backbiter
The woe, v.1, is pronounced on the slanderer or one who speaks evil.

105. The Elephant
Mecca is said once to have been attacked by an army with elephants under the leadership of a certain Abraha, an Ethiopian prince from Yemen. The attack failed because of an epidemic of smallpox which broke out in the army, 1. Muhammad is said to have been born in the precise year in which this happened, 570.

106. Quraysh
This tribe from Mecca, to which Muhammad himself also belonged, is mentioned in the first verse.

107. Charity
Verse 7 tells of those who refuse charity (recompense others with violence).

108. Abundance
Verse 1 speaks of the abundance which God has given. This is the shortest *surah*, consisting of ten words

109. The Unbelievers
The first verse addresses unbelievers.

110. Help

The first verse speaks of God's help.

This is the last chapter, which was revealed three months before Muhammad's death.

111. Fibres

The fibres round the neck of the wife of Muhammad's uncle Abu Lahab, who was and remained a notorious opponent of Muhammad.

112. Sincere Religion

The word which forms the title does not occur in the Qur'an. This chapter is also known as the chapter on 'unity'. *Ikhlas* means making worship pure for God. It can be translated uprightness. In the Qur'an it means pure monotheistic faith (that of a *hanif*, as Abraham is called) by comparison with that of the polytheists. By introducing other gods one makes worship unclean; cf. 39.2, 4, 11, 12, 13, 14 (14, 16, 17); 38.45, 46.

113. Daybreak

The title refers to the first light that breaks through.

This and the next chapters are called the chapters about 'seeking refuge' and are used as formulae to ward off evil. On various occasions in the Qur'an people are called on to seek refuge with God, 7.200 (199); 41.36; 19.18; 23.97; 98 (99,100).

114. Men

Verse 1 speaks of seeking refuge with the 'Lord of men'.

Passages to look up

It would be useful to leaf through the Qur'an with the help of this survey to get a first impression of the order and arrangement of the themes to be discussed. This will help you to gain initial familiarity with the Qur'an as a whole. Perhaps then also the difference in style between the longer and shorter chapters will be apparent, a difference that also clearly comes out in the translations.

3

Muhammad and Revelation

'Say: "I am only a mortal the like of you; it is revealed to me that your God is One God,"' 18.110.

'It is He who has sent His Messenger with the guidance and the religion of truth, that He may uplift it above every religion. God suffices as a witness. Muhammad is the Messenger of God, and those who are with him are hard against the unbelievers, merciful one to another,' 48.28, 29.

'By the Star when it plunges,
your comrade is not astray, neither errs,
nor speaks he out of caprice.
This is naught but a revelation revealed,' 53.1–4.

Introduction

If we want to understand the content of the Qur'an to any degree we need to get to know the Prophet Muhammad and the main events of his life (see Appendix 2). One of the most important and reliable sources for his biography is the Qur'an itself.

In this chapter I shall mention some of the earliest information about his life and also discuss above all the beginning of the descent of the revelations. I shall try to show how the Qur'an speaks about Muhammad's first appearance as a prophet and his calling. That the revelation took place in Arabic was for Muhammad himself a special sign of its reliability and authenticity.

Alongside the revelation that the prophet Muhammad and the other prophets before him received, God revealed himself in 'natural' signs (*ayat*). Both the verbal and non-verbal revelations are called signs. The same term is also used for each separate verse of the Qur'an.

The young Muhammad

Muhammad is said to have been born in the year of the elephant. This must have been around 570. In that particular year the Abyssinian ruler of Yemen, Abraha, led a campaign against the Ka'ba in Mecca, a sanctuary which already existed in the pre-Islamic period. The city was not taken because an epidemic of plague broke out in his army. One of the older chapters of the Qur'an, 105, alludes to this event.

'Hast thou not seen how thy Lord did with the Men of the Elephant?

Did He not make their guile to go astray? And He loosed upon them birds in flights, hurling against them stones of baked clay and He made them like green blades devoured,' 105.1–5.

Muhammad was born in Mecca in quite needy circumstances. His father, 'Abdallah, had already died before his birth. When Muhammad was around a year old, his mother, Amina, also died. So having lost his father, he rapidly became an orphan. His grandfather 'Abd al-Muttalib, and later his uncle Abu Talib, looked after him. After leading a number of caravans for Khadiyah, at the age of twenty-five Muhammad married this widow of a merchant, who was around fifteen years older. This led to an improvement in his social and economic position. These facts, which are known from tradition, form the background to what is written in one of the earliest parts of the Qur'an:

'Did He (God) not find thee (Muhammad) an orphan, and shelter thee?
Did He not find thee erring, and guide thee?
Did He not find thee needy and suffice thee?,' 93.6–8.

Muhammad came from the Quraysh tribe, which was the leading tribe in Mecca, but he himself belonged to an impoverished branch of these aristocratic traders. In the surroundings in which he grew up there was not much religion, at least in the deeper sense of the word. There was some worship of holy places and stones, like the black stone which to the present day forms part of cube-shaped Ka'ba in Mecca.

In Medina, a city around one hundred and twenty miles north of Mecca, there lived some Jewish tribes who had possibly gone there after the fall of Jerusalem in the year 70 CE. There was no Christian church or community in Mecca, but there were itinerant Christian preachers and also monks in the wilderness, hermits and anchorites, cf. 22.40 (41); 5.82 (85). It is related that Muhammad once heard such a preacher preaching in one of the markets. Thus there is a story that on one of his caravan trips to Syria Muhammad met a Christian monk called Bahira. The place where this said to have happened, in Bosra in the south of Syria, is still pointed out.

Prophetic awakening

Muhammad became discontented with both the religious and social situation of his fellow-townsmen. He got the feeling that Arabia had been forgotten by God. *God Passed By Eboli* is the title of a book about the wretched situation in southern Italy. Muhammad felt the same thing: Arabia was a part of the world forgotten by God. Whereas other people had received messengers, the Arabians had been deprived of such care from God.

Muhammad was offended at the growing social injustice in his home city. The extreme wealth of some merchants stood in stark contrast to the blatant poverty of those who were exploited by them.

Muhammad had the habit of going regularly to a cave, Hira, near Mecca. There he had the experience of hearing the voice of God.

Just as Isaiah once heard, 'A voice says, "Cry",' and asked 'What shall I cry?' (Isaiah 40.6), so Muhammad heard a voice which says 'Speak', and asked, 'What shall I speak?' The angel said:

> 'Recite: In the name of thy Lord who created, created Man of a blood-clot. Recite: And thy Lord is the Most Generous, who taught by the Pen, taught Man, that he knew not,' 96.1–4.

This experience must have been very emotional for Muhammad. Trembling, he sought solace with his wife Khadiya. She plays an important part in confirming him in his role as Prophet. Above all when for a time no further revelations came to him, he was in crisis. Muhammad seems even to have been so shocked that for a moment he considered committing suicide.

> 'If We willed, We could take away that We have revealed to thee, then thou wouldst find none thereover to guard thee against Us, excepting by some mercy of thy Lord; surely His favour to thee is great,' 17.86, 87 (88, 89); cf. 28.46.

We can discover from the descriptions in the oldest chapters of the Qur'an that the process which preceded Muhammad's prophetic awakening was not easy.

> '. . . taught him by one terrible in power, very strong,' 53.5.

> 'Behold, we shall cast upon thee a weighty word,' 73.5.

> 'Did We not expand thy breast for thee and lift from thee thy burden, the burden that weighed down thy back?,' 94.1–3.

This last verse is later developed into a legend which tells how the angel Gabriel opened Muhammad's breast and cleansed his heart of sin when he was still a child; cf. 20.25 (26); 7.2.

After an interruption which perhaps lasted six months, the revelations began again.

How does the Qur'an describe these experiences, experiences which also happened to other prophets in the visions that they had at their call (cf. Isaiah 6; Jeremiah 1.9,10; Ezekiel 1 and Revelation 1.9–19)?

Did God himself speak to Muhammad, appear to him or did he speak indirectly to him by a messenger or an angel? Did Muhammad really see God?

The following passage is often cited as a description of his call:

> 'Behold, We sent it (i.e. the Qur'an, although part of the Qur'an and not the whole Qur'an will be meant) down in the Night of Power; And what shall teach thee what is the Night of Power? The Night of Power is better than a thousand months; in it the angels and the Spirit descend, by the leave of their Lord . . .,' 97.1–4.

'We sent this (book) down in a blessed night,' it is said elsewhere, 44.3 (2), a clear allusion to the same event. It is also possible that this event took place during the month of Ramadan:

> 'The month of Ramadan, wherein the Qur'an was sent down to be a guidance,' 2.185 (181).

As I have said, this probably does not mean the sending down of the whole of the Qur'an but the beginning of this revelation, an experience which remained so decisive and normative for Muhammad despite all the later revelations. The Islamic tradition has given the twenty-seventh day of the month Ramadan as the night in which the first descent took place.

Khadiya comforted and encouraged Muhammad and wrapped him (or he wrapped himself) in a mantle. Muhammad heard the words:

> 'O thou shrouded in thy mantle, arise, and warn (your fellow-citizens of the punishment of God)! Thy Lord magnify, thy robes purify, and defilement flee! Give not, thinking to gain greater and be patient unto thy Lord,' 74.1–6.

Here Muhammad is commanded to get up, while another passage, 73.2, says that he has to get up *in the night*. This could be an indication that Muhammad's first experience of revelation took place in the night.

Muhammad could have regarded the event in which he experienced God's presence and his care as a kind of private experience and only as a personal comfort in his time of need. However, it went much further. Just as the prophet Jeremiah is told that God will make him powerful, 'You are too strong for me and have overcome me', Jeremiah 2.7, so the word of God becomes so powerful for Muhammad that he must speak. He is compelled to warn his people and therefore there follows the part of the Qur'an quoted earlier, which speaks about his personal experience of salvation, help and refuge.

'As for the orphan, do not oppress him, and as for the beggar, scold him not; and as for thy Lord's blessing, declare it,' 93.9–11.

Muhammad did this all his life, from about 610 until the 'emigration' to Mecca in 622, and from this time to his death in Medina in 632.

What Muhammad saw and heard
A description is given in different places in this Qur'an of precisely what Muhammad saw and heard at the first revelations.

'By the Star when it plunges, your comrade (i.e. Muhammad) is not astray, neither errs, nor speaks he out of caprice.
This (Qur'an) is naught but a revelation revealed, taught him by one terrible in power, very strong; he stood poised, being on the higher horizon, then drew near and suspended hung, two bows'-length away, or nearer, then revealed to his servant that he revealed.
His heart lies not of what he saw;
what, will you dispute with him (Muhammad) what he sees?
Indeed, he saw him another time by the Lote-Tree of the Boundary nigh which is the Garden of the Refuge,
when there covered the Lote-tree that which covered;
his eye swerved not, nor swept astray.
Indeed, he saw one of the greatest signs of his Lord,' 53.1–18.

It seems that the presupposition here is (still) that Muhammad in fact saw God himself. But other passages in the Qur'an clearly speak of Gabriel as the one who communicates the message.

In this passage of the Qur'an two experiences seem to be being described at the same time. In one the prophet sees the angel of revelation at the highest rim or horizon, while on another occasion he sees him by the most distant lotus tree. In both cases the angel descends. This is a spiritual experience and not a physical movement.

'His heart lies not of what he saw,' 53.11.

Another text which can be mentioned in this connection is:

'Truly this is the word (namely, the Qur'an) of a noble Messenger (cf. 69.40) having power, with the Lord of the Throne secure, obeyed, moreover trusty. Your companion is not possessed; he truly saw him on the clear horizon; he is not niggardly of the Unseen,' 81–19–24. (He is not reluctant also to say what he has learned.)

The Qur'an speaks in yet another place as follows about the way in which God sends revelations:

'It belongs not to any mortal that God should speak to him, except

> by revelation, or from behind a veil, or that He should send a messenger (angel) and He reveal whatsoever He will, by His leave; surely he is All-high, All-wise. Even so We have revealed to thee a Spirit of Our bidding (*amr*). Thou knewest not what the Book was, nor belief; but We made it a light, whereby We guide whom We will of Our servants,' 42.51,52 (50–52).

According to a famous tradition someone once asked the Prophet:

'How does the revelation come to you?' He answered: 'Sometimes it comes to me like the ringing of a bell. And this is the most painful manner of revelation to me; then it leaves me and through this sound I have understood what He (God) meant to say.'

What Muhammad is trying to communicate here is that at the moment he receives the revelation he does not have the awareness of having heard any comprehensible spoken words. All that he hears is something mysterious, like an unarticulated sound, but the moment it stops, he is aware that the sound has already transformed itself into different words.

In another chapter of the Qur'an this sending down is connected with the Holy Spirit or Gabriel.

> 'Say: "The Holy Spirit sent it (the Qur'an) down from thy Lord in truth, and to confirm those who believe, and to be a guidance and good tidings to those who surrender,"' 16.102 (104).

The Holy Spirit and the angels are often mentioned in the same breath in the Qur'an, 97.4.

Just as Gabriel is a messenger (*rasul*) sent by God to Muhammad, 81.19, so Muhammad himself is a messenger, an intermediary between God and the world, 81.19.

> 'Said he, "My people, there is no error in me; but I am a Messenger from the Lord of all Being. I deliver to you the Messages of my Lord,"' 7.61, 62 (59, 60).

The words are put in the mouth of Noah, but equally apply to Muhammad himself (cf. chapter 7).

> 'O Messenger, deliver that which has been sent down to thee from thy Lord; for if thou dost not, thou wilt not have delivered His Message,' 5.67 (71).

The message must be remembered well and not distorted or falsified, which is what the Qur'an accuses the Jews of having done. They are said to have distorted the revealed words, 7.117; cf. 2.75–79 (70–73); 3.78 (72); 4.46 (48); 5.13 (16), 41 (45). But Muhammad himself is also warned not to move his tongue in haste, but to follow the revealed sequence of words. For otherwise he himself could have formed the word instead of calmly waiting until the revelation has come to an end.

> 'Move not thy tongue with it to hasten it;
> Ours it is to gather it, and to recite it.
> So, when We recite it, follow thou its recitation.
> Then Ours it is to explain it,' 75.16–19 (and that 'We' refers to God).

Muhammad is not possessed

Above all at the beginning of his activity as a prophet, Muhammad is sometimes afraid and anxious and thinks that he is possessed. He doubts whether the source of the mysterious voice that he hears contains the true message of God.

'The truth is of God; be not of the doubters,' 3.60 (53). (This is said in connection with Jesus, but as often in the stories of the prophets it can also be explained with reference to Muhammad, 3.60 (53).)

> 'Whom We have given the Book, and they recognize it as they recognize their sons, even though there is a party of them conceal the truth and that wittingly. The truth comes from thy Lord; then be not among the doubters,' 2.146, 147 (141, 142).

According to the Qur'an, the source of Muhammad's inspiration is not a *jinn*, but God. There is an absolute difference between the two, for God is the creator of the whole world, whereas the *jinns* are simply created beings, 6.100, and they will be brought before God with men and women on the day of judgment, 37.158.

Muhammad is not a poet. A poet is by nature a liar, 26.222. A soothsayer (*kahin*) was also possessed. Certainly God's revelations to Muhammad are given in a particular rhythmic style and are characterized by strange oaths, adjurations, a genre which also occurs in some of the earliest passages of the Qur'an. But Muhammad is neither.

> 'Therefore remind! By thy Lord's blessing thou art not a soothsayer neither possessed,' 52.29, 30; cf. 69.42.

An Arabic Qur'an

Muhammad's opponents do not believe in the authenticity and reliability of Muhammad's message.

> 'The unbelievers say, "This is naught but a calumny he has forged,

and other folk have helped him (Muhammad) to it." So they have committed wrong and falsehood.

They say, "Fairy-tales of the ancients that he has had written down, so that they are recited to him at the dawn and in the evening."

Say: "He (God) sent it down, who knows the secret in the heavens and earth; He is All-forgiving, All-compassionate,"' 25.4–6 (5–7).

The Qur'an often says that Muhammad's opponents claim that he has been enlightened by human informants about what he presents as the revelation of God. Names of Christian or Jewish persons who could be these informants are mentioned in the Islamic tradition. The Qur'an offers a specific argument against this:

> 'And We know very well that they (the unbelievers) say, "Only a mortal is teaching him." The speech of him at whom they hint is barbarous (i.e., not Arabic); and this is speech Arabic, manifest,' 16.103 (105).

This text sets out to refute the assertion of Muhammad's opponents that Jewish or Christian writings are presented by informants by means of the argument that the opponents speak another language whereas Muhammad uses Arabic as the language of revelation.

It is repeatedly emphasized in the Qur'an that this is an Arabic Qur'an, a book that is revealed in clear Arabic:

> '. . . in a clear, Arabic tongue', 26.195.

> 'We have sent no Messenger (the Qur'an then says) save with the tongue of his people, that he might make all clear to them (his fellow-countrymen),' 14.4.

Just as Moses is given a book in his language, so the Arabian prophet Muhammad is given a book in Arabic, 46.12.

> 'If We had sent it (the Arabic Qur'an) down on a barbarian and he had recited it to them, they would not have believed in it,' 26.198,199.

> 'Truly it is the revelation of the Lord of all Being, brought down by the Faithful Spirit upon thy heart, that thou mayest be one of the warners, in a clear, Arabic tongue,' 26.192–95.

The purpose of sending down the message in the people's own language, for Moses in Hebrew and for Muhammad in Arabic, has to do with its comprehensibility:

> 'We have sent it down as an Arabic Qur'an; haply you will understand,' 12.2; cf. 20.113 (112); 42. 7 (5); 43.3 (2).

Thus the thought is that there is a close connection between community and language.

That does not mean that the Qur'an is meant to legitimate the notion that Arabic is a superior language or that the community of Arabian Muslims is superior.

Certainly the Qur'an says,

> 'You are the best nation ever brought forth to men', 3.110 (106),

but that must be to encourage them and to reject what is wrong.

If it is a question of superiority, then according to the Qur'an this is not the superiority of a particular language or a particular people. The greatest godfearer is the most highly noted.

> 'Surely the noblest among you in the sight of God is the most godfearing of you. God is All-knowing, All-aware,' 49.13.

'Signs' as revelations

It is said of God in the Qur'an that he sends revelations in both a verbal and a non-verbal way. Both are called 'signs'. According to the Qur'an, all kinds of phenomena which perhaps could be understood as purely natural are not so.

> 'Surely in the creation of the heavens (note that the Qur'an very often uses 'heaven' in the plural) and the earth and the alternation of night and day and the ship that runs in the sea with profit to men, and the water God sends down from heaven therewith reviving the earth after it is dead and His scattering abroad in it all manner of crawling thing, and the turning about of the winds and the clouds compelled between heaven and earth – surely there are signs for a people having understanding,' 2.164 (159).

There are many references to these signs in the Qur'an: the alternation of day and night, 3.190 (187); 10.6; 45.5 (4); 23.80 (82); 25.62 (63); the ships that go on the sea, 14.32 (37); 22.65 (64); 45.12 (11); 30.46 (45); 17.66 (68); 31.31 (30); the water from heaven that revives the earth, 16.65 (67); 45.5 (4); 30.24 (23), 19 (18), 50, 49, 29; 63; the animals that are spread over the earth, 31.10 (9); 42.29 (28); 45.4 (3) and the winds and clouds, 45.5 (4); 15.22; 35.9 (10); 7.57 (55).

According to the Qur'an all this must not just be seen as natural phenomena; rather, these phenomena are so many symbols of God's intervention in human affairs, proofs of His providential care and wisdom for the well-being of people on earth. These signs serve to direct people's attention to something that extends further than the phenomena. They are signs which speak of the mighty acts of God. They point to what God does in His benevolence, power, sovereignty and righteousness.

It is obvious that these non-verbal signs are vaguer and more global than the verbal signs, that is, the signs in the form of the verses of the Qur'an. Whereas the non-verbal signs have been given to the whole of humankind without distinction and without mediation, the verbal signs are given to the Prophet, who must hand them on through people.

The God of Whom it is said that He puts signs in nature is the God who sends these signs down in the form of verses of the Qur'an.

The verbal signs can clarify the signs of God in nature.

> 'Behold how We turn about the signs; haply they will understand,' 6.65.

God has clearly expounded these signs for people who have knowledge and understanding, 6.97, 98; cf. also 2.118 (112); 2.219 (217); 2.266 (268); 3.118 (114); 5.75 (79).

It is often said that these verses are recited. They are also called 'clear' proofs to which prophets refer, 11.17 (20), 28 (30), 65 (66), 88 (90); 47.14 (15).

Two reactions are possible to both sorts of signs, acceptance or rejection. They are affirmed as true or regarded as false. They are accepted or they are seen as vain, as products of fantasy. The one attitude leads to belief, the other to unbelief.

The symbolic nature of signs can be understood only by those who have understanding, those who reflect in the true sense of the word. The Qur'an speaks repeatedly of the longing for people to *come to insight*, to *consider*, to *see*. The Qur'an repeatedly asks hearers to *reflect*, 7.184 (183); to take counsel with themselves; 30.8 (7), to ponder the creation of the heavens and the earth, 3.191 (188). The parable of the dog which keeps panting whether you drive it away or let it rest is told for people to reflect on, 7.176 (175). All kinds of (natural) signs are spoken about to make people reflect, 3.118(114); 10.24 (25); 13.3 ;16.11, 69 (71); 45.13 (12). These signs are meant to make people reflect, and that is also the purpose of the signs in the form of the message of revelation, 16.44 (46). The Qur'an also says that these (natural) signs are given to make people *understand*, 2.73 (68); 2.164 (159), 242 (243); 3.4, 118 (114); 16.12, 67 (69); 30.24 (23); 45.5 (4). The signs in the form of verses of the Qur'an are revealed with the same purpose, for people to become understanding, 12.1, cf. 21.10; 43.3 (2).

'Now We have made clear to you the signs, if you understand,' 3.118 (114).

The signs always have the purpose of arousing the feeling of gratitude in the human spirit. That is especially true of the signs which reveal God as the grateful and merciful God. Human beings should show gratitude for these precious gifts.

'And it is God who brought you forth knowing nothing, from your mothers' wombs, and He appointed for you hearing, and sight, and hearts, that haply so you will be thankful,' 16.78 (80).

'And of His signs is that He looses the winds, bearing good tidings and that He may let you taste of His mercy, and that the ships may run at His commandment, and that you may seek His bounty; haply so you will be thankful,' 30.46 (45); cf.45.12 (11); 5.89 (91).

But in the majority of instances the description ends with the complaint that people are so often ungrateful and thus unbelieving.

'God is bountiful to men; but most of them are not thankful,' 10.60 (61); cf. 28.73; 27.73 (75); 2.243 (244); 40.61 (63).

However much God also leads people on the right way, showing sign after sign, if people are not in a position to understand their meaning, then the signs cannot work.

One can understand the divine signs with the heart. But if that is sealed and covered and does not function well, then people do not understand anything at all.

'... and a seal has been set upon their hearts, so they understand not,' 9.87 (88); cf. 63.3; 9.93 (94).

'It is not the eyes that are blind, but blind are the hearts within the breasts,' 22.46 (45); cf. 2.7; 45.23 (22); 6.46; 24.42 (23); 16.108 (110).

If it functions normally, the heart is made to understand these signs. The meaning of the divine signs can be comprehended by an understanding, reflecting and comprehending heart .

Passages to look up

There are two expressions in the Qur'an to denote the 'revelation' which Muhammad and the other messengers received. One can be translated 'inspiration' (*wahy*), the other 'sending down' (*tanzil*).

The first expression (or derivations of it) is found in the following verses: 6.19; 10.2; 12.109; 16.43 (45); 17.86 (88); 21.7, 25, 45 (46); 42.7 (5), 51 (59; 53.4,10).

The second expression is used in the following verses: 2.4 (3), 97 (91), 136 (130); 3.84 (78); 4.60 (63), 162 (160); 5.59 (64); 10.37 (38); 16.102 (104); 26.192; 29.46 (45); 32.2; 36.5 (4); 39.1; 40.2; 41.2, 42; 45.2; 46.2; 56.80 (79); 9.43; 6.26 (also including passages where belief in what is 'sent down' is mentioned).

Although the Qur'an alludes numerous times to Muhammad, his name is actually mentioned only a few times, 3.144 (138); 33.40; 47.2; 48.29. Possibly 'Ahmad is also to be understood as a reference to the name of Muhammad, 61.6.

To get an impression of the place that Muhammad accepts in his own community at the end of his life, see the following verses:

The Qur'an shows the special place of Muhammad above others, 33.6. People are asked to say blessings on Muhammad, 33.56.

The Qur'an regulates how one has to behave towards Muhammad, 33.53(-59). A certain etiquette is prescribed, 24.62; 58.11 (12). If one is in a position to, one must give a loving gift for a meeting with the Prophet, 58.12,13 (13,14). Conversation with the Prophet must not be in a loud voice, 49.1–5 (especially 2.3).

The Qur'an regulates what marital relationships are specially allowed for Muhammad, 33.50–52 (49–52). The Qur'an regulates particular problems which arise in Muhammad's harem, 66.1–5.

After his death the widows of Muhammad may not remarry, 33.53.

4

God

'God, there is no god but He, the Living, the Everlasting. Slumber seizes Him not, neither sleep; to Him belongs all that is in the heavens and the earth. Who is there that shall intercede with Him save by His leave? He knows what lies before them and what is after them, and they comprehend not anything of His knowledge save such as He wills. His Throne comprises the heavens and earth; the preserving of them oppresses Him not; He is the All-high, the All-glorious,' 2.255 *(256).*

(This so-called 'throne verse' is often depicted in Kufic or other calligraphic writing on tombstones).

Introduction

It was once said of Muhammad that he was 'God intoxicated'. That amounts to saying that he was 'possessed by God'. Allah's name occurs 2,500 times in the Qur'an. A name which is also used often is 'Lord' (*rabb*) and the divine name 'Compassionate' (*Rahman*). God is the 'subject' of the Qur'an. Everything that is related in the Qur'an turns on what He reveals, says and asks of people . . . God has kept some things hidden and revealed others. According to the Qur'an, God's name must be praised. Allah is addressed in the Qur'an with many 'beautiful' names or attributes, as Islamic theology will later put it. The Qur'an emphasizes that God the True One is the Creator. A special characteristic of Qur'anic talk of God is also that God is One. In connection with this last word, the story is told that Muhammad once wanted to make a concession to his polytheistic fellow-townsmen on this point.

God and secrecy

At the beginning of the second chapter of the Qur'an we read:

> 'That is the Book, wherein is no doubt, (revealed as) a guidance to the godfearing who believe in the Unseen,' 2.1, 3; cf. 5.94 (95); 21.49 (50); 35.18 (19); 36.11 (10); 50.33 (32); 57.25; 67.12.

To some degree the revelation of God has made this unseen, this hidden One visible, although the Qur'an also makes it clear that:

'The eyes attain Him not, but He attains the eyes,' 6.103.

The revelation is revealed to some, like the prophets.

> 'He (Muhammad) is not niggardly of the Unseen,' 81.24; cf. 68.47; 52.41; 53.35 (36); 12.102 (103); 11.49 (51).

> 'Knower He of the Unseen, and He discloses not His Unseen to anyone,' 72.26.

> 'He is God; there is no god but He. He is the knower of the Unseen and the Visible; He is the All-merciful, the All-compassionate,' 59.22; cf. 64.18; 49.18; 39.46 (47); 35.38 (36); 32.6 (5); 23.92 (94); 18.26 (25); 16.77 (79); 13.9 (10); 11.31 (33); 7.188.

Certainly knowledge can be brought near to those who reflect. The Qur'an says that they get to paradise.

> 'Whoever fears the All-merciful in the Unseen, and comes with a penitent heart,' 50.33 (32).

Praising God

Time and again man is called on in the Qur'an to praise God. Perhaps the first six verses of chapter 57 are the finest example of this. The praise at the same time expresses what He who needs to be praised does.

> 'All that is in the heavens and the earth magnifies God; He is the All-mighty, the All-wise.
> To Him belongs the Kingdom of the heavens and the earth; He gives life, and He makes to die, and He is powerful over everything.
> He is the First and the Last, the Outward and the Inward; He has knowledge of everything.
> It is He that created the heavens and the earth in six days then seated Himself upon the Throne.
> He knows what penetrates into the earth, and what comes forth from it, and what comes down from heaven, and what goes up unto it. He is with you wherever you are; and God sees the things you do. To Him belongs the Kingdom of the heavens and the earth; and unto Him all matters are returned. He makes the night to enter into the day and makes the day to enter into the night. He knows the thoughts within the breasts,' 57.1–6.

The beautiful names

In popular Islam worship it is customary to use the *subha* – a kind of rosary. In its Muslim version this rosary – which is of Buddhist origin and spread into mediaeval Europe via the Islamic world, has either ninety-nine or thirty-three beads. Although this rosary is of course also customarily used as worry beads, its religious function is to help the believer to think of the ninety-nine 'beautiful names' of God.

> 'To God belong the Names Most Beautiful; so call Him by them,' 7.180 (179); cf. 17.110; 20.8 (7); 59.24.

Nowhere does the Qur'an give the number of names of God. The number ninety-nine came into being with the understanding that the hundredth name is Allah. The so-called ninety-nine names are primarily but not exclusively taken from the Qur'an. There are names in the series of ninety-nine which do not occur in the Qur'an and there are names which occur in the Qur'an but are not part of the so-called ninety-nine.

I do not want to sum up all the names here, but it can be said that in the Qur'an God is preached as the Creator of heaven and earth and of man. It is also he who gives guidance to man: 'He guides whom he will on the right way' and it is also he who will judge individuals and peoples in strict justice (thus not like a capricious judge) and with a judgment that is characterized by fairness. At the same time, it is constantly repeated, God is the merciful.

> 'God has prescribed for himself mercy,' 6.12.

> 'His mercy embraces all things,' 7.156 (155).

God is described as one, forgiving, merciful, as the one who speaks.

God cannot be seen without a veil, at least not in this world. God can be known only though His signs.

In the period before the coming of Islam God was not wholly unknown among the Arabians under the name of Allah. The name of Muhammad's father, ʿAbdallah, which means 'servant of Allah', already indicates this.

But the Qur'an itself states emphatically:

> 'If thou askest them (the reference is to the pagan Arabians), 'Who created the heavens and the earth and subjected the sun and the moon?," they will say, "God" (Allah),' 9.61.

> 'If thou askest them, "Who sends down out of heaven water, and therewith revives the earth after it is dead?," they will say, "God,"' 29.63.

Oaths were clearly sworn by the name of God (Allah) in the pre-Islamic period, 35.42 (40); 16.38 (40).

God is true
In the Qur'an God is described as the one who alone is true:

> 'That is because God – He is the Truth, and that they call apart from Him – that is the false,' 22.62 (61); cf. 31.30 (29).

This verse expresses the vanity of the idols. They are only inventions of human whim, unfounded fables and mere names. Over against them stands the reality and the truth of God. God is at work in the process of the life of the world and of all that exists. He brings the dead back to life and he has the power to restore nature to true life.

> 'That is because God – He is the Truth, and brings the dead to life, and is powerful over everything,' 22.6.

The quality of this reality is understood above all in terms of His great creative activity:

> 'Say: "Who provides you out of heaven and earth, or who possesses hearing and sight, and who brings forth the living from the dead and brings forth the dead from the living, and who directs the affair?" They will surely say, "God." Then say: "Will you not be godfearing?" That then is God, your Lord, the True; what is there, after truth, but error?,' 10.31, 32 (32, 33); cf. 3.27 (26); 30.19.

God the creator
The Qur'an is regarded as one great hymn in honour of the divine creation. The Qur'an is permeated through and through with the notion of creation by God and a feeling of deep wonderment at it. Man is constantly called on to be aware of his creatureliness and to be grateful to God for his goodness and to honour Him. The creation bears witness to God's power.

Just as God (Allah) was not completely unknown to the Arabians before the coming of Islam, so Muhammad clearly thinks that his opponents believe in God as creator, 29.61–63; 31.25 (24):

> 'If thou askest them, "Who created the heavens and the earth?" they will say, "God." Say: "What think you? That you call upon apart from God – if God desires affliction for me, shall they remove His affliction? Or if He desires mercy for me, shall they withhold His mercy?" Say: "God is enough for me; in Him all those put their trust who put their trust," ' 39.38 (39).

The charge that Muhammad makes against his opponents is that they do not draw the necessary consequences from this belief in God the creator:

'And the most part of them believe not in God, but they associate other gods with Him,' 12.106; cf. 43.87; 43.9 (8); 40.12.

God is the creator of the whole world: of the angels, 43.19 (18); the *jinns*, 55.15 (14); the heavens and the earth, 14.19 (22); the sun and the moon, the day and the night, 41.37; the mountains and the rivers, 13.3; the trees, the fruits, the grain and the vegetation, 55.11, 12 (10, 11); all kinds of creatures: those who go on their bellies, two-footed and four-footed, 24.45 (44). In short He is the creator of everything, 6.102; 13.16 (17). He creates what He wills, 42.49 (48); through His command what He says comes into being. Here one could also think of the biblical parallels where for example it is also said, 'For He spoke and it was there; He commanded and it existed' (Psalm 33.9).

God's word of power and His command bring existence into being. Whenever God wants something, He has only to say 'Become' and it becomes, 36.52:

'The only words We say to a thing, when We desire it, is that We say to it "Be", and it is,' 16.40.

'. . . and when He decrees a thing, He but says to it "Be", and it is,' 2.117(111)

'It is He who gives life, and makes to die; and when He decrees a thing, He but says to it "Be", and it is,' 40.68 (70).

This notion of God's creative capacity also defines what is said about Jesus in the Qur'an. Mary asks the angel how she can have a child when she is not married:

'"Lord," said Mary, "'how shall I have a son seeing no mortal has touched me?" "Even so," God said, "God creates what He will. When he decrees a thing He does but say to it 'Be', and it is,"' 3.47 (42).

'It is not for God to take a son unto Him. Glory be to Him! When He decrees a thing, He but says to it "Be", and it is,' 19.35 (36).

The Qur'an makes it clear that this creating is not whimsical, a game or something to pass the time. It would not be compatible with the power of the almighty God and the compassion of the Compassionate One for Him to do something like this:

'. . . there are signs for men possessed of minds who remember God, standing and sitting and on their sides, and reflect upon the creation of the heavens and the earth: (they say,) "Our Lord, Thou hast not created this for vanity,"' 3.191 (188); cf. 38.27 (26); 44.38,39; 6.73 (72).

'We created not the heaven and the earth and whatsoever between them is, as playing; had We desired to take to Us a diversion We would have taken it to Us from Ourselves, had We done aught,' 21.16,17; cf. 15.85; 46.3 (2); 30.8 (7).

In focussing on the creation of human beings the Qur'an opposes the idea that this was nonsensical and purposeless:

'What, did you think that We created you only for sport, and that you would not be returned to Us?', 23.115, 116 (117).

'What, does man reckon he shall be left to roam at will?,' 75.36.

The unity of God

Quite central to the Qur'an is the confession 'There is no God but God.' It is related of one of the most important opponents of Muhammad, 'Umar ibn al-Khattab, that he once heard chapter 73 of the Qur'an read. This contains the sentence 'There is no God but God' (v.7). When that happened he was converted. Because of his powerful conversion, this initially fervent opponent of Muhammad who then became an equally fiery supporter is compared with Paul.

According to some, the whole essence of the Qur'an is summed up in these words 'there is no God but God'. Just as the confession 'Hear, Israel, the Lord is our God, the Lord is one' in Deuteronomy 6.4 is central to Judaism, so this confession of the unity of God is central for Muslims. That is expressed in one of the earliest chapters of the Qur'an:

'Say: "He is God, One,
God, the Everlasting Refuges,
who has not begotten, and has not been begotten,
and equal to Him is not any one,"' 112.1–4.

Every Muslim knows this text by heart. It is written in calligraphy in many mosques. God is also called 'the Eternal One', *Samad*. That word means something like immovable, indestructible rock, a firm refuge against floods. Anyone who bases themselves on less than this rock, as the Qur'an calls it, becomes a loser, 39.15 (17); 11.21 (23), because he prefers something as fragile as a spider's web:

'The likeness of those who have taken to them protectors, apart from

God, is as the likeness of the spider that takes to itself a house; and surely the frailest of houses is the house of the spider, did they but know,' 29.41.

Chapter 112, quoted above, is often heard as an implicit rejection of Christian belief in Jesus as Son of God, but that was certainly not the case originally. In the early period from which this chapter comes, Muhammad is opposing the polytheism of his fellow-townsmen, cf. further 6.19; 16.22 (23), 51 (53); 22.34 (35); 37.4; and the associated thought that God has sons or daughters. This chapter, which is called 'dedication' (*ikhlas*), unconditional faith, expresses the deepest Muslim attitude, namely that of someone who directs all his faith to God, 4.146 (145).

God is one:

'Had God desired to take to Him a son, He would have chosen whatever He willed of that He has created. Glory be to Him!
He is God, the One, the Omnipotent,' 39.4 (6); 40.16; 14.48 (49); cf. 13.16 (17).

It is argued against the Meccans, who attribute sons and daughters to God, that 'Your God is one', 37.4. That is constantly repeated not only in the Meccan but also in the Medinan period, 2.163 (158). The unity of God is a quite central point in Muhammad's preaching, as is repeatedly stated:

'Say: "I am only a mortal the like of you; it is revealed to me that your God is One God. So let him, who hopes for the encounter with his Lord, work righteousness, and not associate with his Lord's service anyone,' 18.110.

'It is revealed unto me only that your God is One God; do you then surrender?,' 21.108.

'Say: "I am only a mortal, like you are. To me it has been revealed that your God is One God; so go straight with Him, and ask for His forgiveness; and woe to the idolaters,"' 41.6 (5).

The unity of God is contrasted with the polytheism of Muhammad's fellow-townsman. The main sin is to give God a consort, to have a partner alongside God. The thought that anyone can have faith in or show loyalty to something or someone outside or alongside God is rejected. In other words, that loyalty which is due to God alone cannot be shown to a particular idol (today we would say ideology). Only God has existence and reality. The rest is nothing:

'Your God is One God; there is no god but He, the All-merciful, the All-compassionate,' 2.163(158).

'God. There is no god but He, the Living, the Everlasting. Slumber seizes Him not, neither sleep (cf. Psalm121), to Him belongs all that is in the heavens and the earth,' 2.255 (256).

'God. There is no god but He, the Living, the Everlasting, 3.2; cf. 3.6 (4).

'God bears witness that there is no god but He,' 3.18 (14); cf. 4.87 (89); 6.102,106.

'There is no God but He. He gives life and makes to die. Believe then in God, and in His Messenger, the Prophet of the common folk, who believes in God and His words, and follow him; haply so you will be guided,' 7.158.

This verse calls on God and Muhammad to believe. Belief in the unity of God implies that no other can be worshipped or believed in as God and Lord.

The Qur'an accuses the Jews of having made Ezra son of God and the Christians of having made the Messiah son of God:

'They have taken their rabbis and their monks as lords apart from God, and the Messiah, Mary's son – and they were commanded to serve but One God; there is no god but He; glory be to Him, above that they associate,' 9.30,31.

Such faith gives certainty:

'So if they turn their backs, say: "God is enough for me. There is no god but He. In Him I have put my trust. He is the Lord of the Mighty Throne,"' 9.129 (130).

According to the Qur'an all prophets before Muhammad left no doubt in their preaching about the unity of God:

'And We never sent a Messenger before thee except that We revealed to him, saying, "There is no god but I; so serve Me,"' 21.25.

This is also said by Moses in 20.14:

'Verily I am God; there is no god but I.'

Thus the children of Israel believe that there is no God than He.

According to the Qur'an one could say that they thus adhere to a Muslim confession of faith, although they are not Muslims in the sociological sense of the word.

This is certainly an indication of how the Qur'an always gives the religion of the Jews and indeed that of the Christians an Islamic colouring. The belief of Jews and Christians is understood in Muslim terms; cf. 11.4 (17):

> 'Thus We (God) have sent thee among a nation before which other nations have passed away, to recite to them that We have revealed to thee; and yet they disbelieve in the All-merciful. Say: "He is my Lord – there is no god but He. In Him I have put my trust, and to Him I turn,"' 13.30 (29).

For Muhammad, belief in God, who alone is God, and not trusting in another God go together; cf. 16.2; 20.8 (7); 14.98 (Moses); 21.25; 27.26 (Solomon); 28.70; 35.3; 37.35 (34); 39.6 (8); 40.3, 62 (64), 65, (67); 44.8 (7); 47.19 (21); 59.22, 23; 64.13; 74.9.

Is the preaching of the unity of God compromised?

Because of the centrality in the Qur'an of belief that God is one and God alone, the story that Muhammad once almost made a concession at this point is all the more telling. The story is connected with chapter 53 of the Qur'an and is handed down by various Islamic sources.

The Quryashi believe in a number of gods. They attribute partners, sons or daughters, to God. The names of some of these are Al-Lat, Al-'Uzza and Manat.

In the Islamic tradition it is related that when the Qurayshi avoided Muhammad and spoke badly of him to his followers, he remarked: 'I wish that something was revealed that kept them from me.' Then once when he was sitting near the Ka'ba in their company, he recited chapter 53 until he came to verses 19 and 20:

> 'Have you considered Al-Lat and Al-'Uzza and Manat the third, the other?', 53.9, 20.

After that he is said to have recited: 'These are the exalted *gharaniq* (herons), and see hope is pinned on their promise.'

According to this story Muhammad repeated the chapter to the end. When he had done this, the whole people bowed in prayer.

In other words, after this concession Muhammad becomes acceptable to the Qurasyhi, as soon as he seemed ready to give a place to their goddesses alongside God. 'If you give a portion to our goddesses, we stand at your side.'

However, the story goes on that as soon as Muhammad got home, the angel Gabriel said to him: 'Did I deliver these words to you?' Then Muhammad answered: 'I have said about God what he is not.' Muhammad is led to see that Satan had revealed these verses to him. Salman Rushdie took the title of his book *The Satanic Verses* from this thought.

After that God revealed to him what is to be found in the Qur'an:

> 'Indeed they were near to seducing thee from that We revealed to thee, that thou mightest forge against Us another (than the Qur'an), and then they would surely have taken thee as a friend; and had We not confirmed thee, surely thou wert near to inclining unto them a very little,' 17.73, 74 (75,76).

Now the Qur'an speaks of the possibility that Satan intervenes in the process of revelation:

> 'We sent not ever any Messenger or Prophet before thee, but that Satan cast into his fancy, when he was fancying; but God annuls what Satan casts, then God confirms His signs – surely God is All-knowing, All-wise,' 22.52 (51).

It becomes clear from the whole of the Qur'an that the notion that God could have sons and above all daughters has been rejected absolutely. There is a certain irony when it is said that Muhammad's opponents themselves like to have male descendants and then attribute daughters to God:

> 'And when any of them is given the good tidings of a girl, his face is darkened and he chokes inwardly,' 16.58 (60).

> 'And they assign to God daughters; glory be to Him! – and they have their desire,' 16.57 (59).

> 'Or has He daughters, and they sons?,' 52.39.

> 'What, have you males, and He females?,' 53.21.

> 'Or has He taken to Himself, from that He creates, daughters, and favoured you with sons?,' 43.16 (15); 37.149.

The answer to the question about the goddesses Al-Lat, Al-'Uzza and Manat is now answered in the Qur'an like this:

> 'They are naught but names yourselves have named, and your fathers; God has sent down no authority touching them. They follow

only surmise, and what the souls desire; and yet guidance has come to them from their Lord,' 53.23.

It is inconceivable that this story which has been handed down by Islamic sources should be made up. Therefore it confirms all the more the importance of the unity of God in the preaching of Muhammad. This insight argues for the trustworthiness of the Prophet Muhammad.

Passages to look up

The praise of God is spoken of various times in the Qur'an. According to the Qur'an those who take part in it are heaven and earth, 17.43, 44 (45, 46); the angels, 39.75; and the birds, 24.41; cf. 43.9–14 (8–13); 59.1, (22-)24; 57.1; 61.1; 62.1; 64.21; 23.28 (29).

Also 1.2; 37.182; 6.1, 45; 7.43 (41); 10.10; 14.39; 15.98; 17.111; 20.130; 50.39 (38); 23.28 (29), etc.

The Qur'an also speaks 'anthropomorphically' about God. Thus there is mention of His hands, with which He has created, 36.71; 38.75 among other things the heaven and the earth, 51.47,58. In His hand is goodness, 3.26 (25). At the last judgment God rolls up the heavens in His right hand, 39.67.

The Qur'an speaks about God's face. Everything shall pass away except for His face, 28.88; cf. 55.27; 2.115 (109). There is mention of longing for God's face, 6.52; 13.22; 18.28 (27); 30.38, 39 (37, 38).

5

The Preaching of the Last Judgment

'We indeed created man; and We know what his soul whispers within him, and We are nearer to him than the jugular vein.

When the two angels meet together, sitting one on the right, and one on the left, not a word he utters, but by him is an observer ready. And death's agony comes in truth; that is what thou wast shunning! And the trumpet shall be blown; that is the day of the Threat. And every soul shall come, and with it a driver and a witness,' 50.16–21 (15–20).

'Decked out fair to men is the love of lusts – women, children, heaped-up heaps of gold and silver, horses of mark, cattle and tillage. That is the enjoyment of the present life; but God – with Him is the fairest resort. Say: "Shall I tell you of a better than that?" For those that are godfearing, with their Lord are gardens underneath which rivers flow, therein dwelling forever, and spouses purified, and God's good pleasure. And God sees His servants,' 3.14,15 (12, 13).

Introduction

The last judgment is one of the themes that are dominant in the Qur'an. Certainly in the initial period of Muhammad's activity, preaching about the approaching judgment played an important role. This message was presented in a climate in which according to Muhammad's fellow townsmen everything will be irrevocably over with death: there is no resurrection of the dead and therefore no judgment on what people have done in life. For them *Carpe diem* was the highest wisdom. Over against that Muhammad sets the preaching about the coming Hour; the day will certainly dawn on which God as judge will pass his verdict and give a reckoning. The Qur'an gives a lively description of this coming event in fierce colours. It spells out in a very outspoken way what reward and punishment will be distributed in heaven or in hell. The Qur'an clearly indicates why people go to heaven or to hell.

This life alone?

Many of Muhammad's fellow-townsmen in Mecca received the message about an approaching judgment with due scepticism, unbelief and mockery. They did not believe that there was anything after this life; there was no resurrection and therefore no final reckoning either.

The resurrection from the dead is a condition for the associated thought of the judgment on the last day:

> 'Who shall quicken the bones when they are decayed,' 36.78.

The people of Mecca found such a notion nonsensical and unthinkable. They dismissed this preaching as old fables, 83.73, and as confused dreams. 21.5. If something of the sort were to happen that would be sheer witchcraft, 11.7 (10):

> 'And they say, "There is only our present life; we shall not be raised,"' 6.29.

> 'There is nothing but our first death; We shall not be revived,' 44.35 (34).

> 'They said, "What, when we are dead and become dust and bones, shall we be indeed raised up? We and our fathers have been promised this before; this is naught but the fairy-tales of the ancients,"' 23.81, 83 (84, 85); cf. 17.49 (52), 98 (100); 37.16, 53 (51); 56.47 (46, 47).

> '... and the unbelievers say, "This is a marvellous thing! What, when we are dead and become dust? That is a far returning,"' 50.2,3.

> 'The unbelievers say, "Shall we point you to a man who will tell you, when you have been utterly torn to pieces, then you shall be in a new creation?,"' 34.7.

According to the people of Mecca, in other words, it is clearly all up with death, cf.23.37 (39); 76.1.

> 'There is nothing but our present life; We die, and we live, and nothing but Time (*dahr*) destroys us,' 45.24 (23).

That last element, 'time', is something mysterious in the pre-Islamic period, something fatalistic that exercises a tyrannical power over the life of men and women.

Thus initially with his preaching Muhammad enters a climate in which there is no belief in a future life and last judgment, but everything is staked on this life. What he sees around him is simply frivolity and pleasure-seeking.

As the Qur'an tells them:

> 'The present life is naught but a sport and a diversion; surely the Last

Abode is better for those that are godfearing. What, do you not understand?,' 6.32; cf. 29.64; 17.36 (38); 57.20 (19).

'Leave alone those who take their religion for a sport and a diversion, and whom the present life has deluded,' 6.70 (69).

'. . . the unbelievers who have taken their religion as a diversion and a sport, and whom the present life has deluded,' 7.51 (49).

'Nay, but you prefer the present life; and the world to come is better, and more enduring,' 87.16, 17.

'You desire the chance goods of the present world, and God desires the world to come,' 8.67 (68).

'They rejoice in this present life; and this present life, beside the world to come, is naught but passing enjoyment,' 13.26; cf. 17.30 (32); 28.92; 29.62; 34.36 (35); 39 (38); 52 (53); 42.12.

'Wealth and sons are the adornment of the present world; but the abiding things, the deeds of righteousness, are better with God in reward, and better in hope,' 18.46 (44).

It is clear that in Muhammad's preaching quite a different picture is given of the human condition from the sombre and fatalistic one which existed before the coming of Islam in Arabia. Suddenly as it were the air clears, the darkness of fate is driven away and in place of the tragic sense of life there appears the prospect of eternal life. The God who is preached is not 'time' (*dahr*), fate, but a God of justice who does no evil. Everything, the whole hope of the life of human beings and the world stands under the control of the will of God.

The term

Of course the reality of material death remains:

'Wherever you may be, death will overtake you,
though you should be in raised-up towers,' 4.78 (80).

Even the prophet Muhammad will not escape death:

'We have not assigned to any mortal before thee to live forever; therefore, if thou diest, will they live forever? Every soul shall taste of death,' 21.34, 35 (35,36); cf.3.185 (182); 29.57.

This last is the case because according to the Qur'an God has assigned a given date for everyone's death:

'We have decreed among you Death,' 56.60.

'God gives life and death.
He gives life, and makes to die,' 9.116 (117).

The term is determined by God:

'It is He who created you of clay, then determined a term and a term is stated with Him,' 6.2.

'It is not given to any soul to die, save by the leave of God, at an appointed time,' 3.145 (139).

But the 'term' does not have the dark colours which hang round the belief of the pre-Islamic period. Death is the transition to the future life. Just as every individual has his term, so too does the world: the 'hour', the day of judgment', is the ultimate term for that.

For those for whom life in the present is everything and who are therefore led astray comes the preaching of judgment with the torments and punishments that are associated with it:

'Upon the day when the unbelievers are exposed to the Fire: "You dissipated your good things in your present life, and you took your enjoyment in them; therefore today you shall be recompensed with the chastisement of humiliation for that you waxed proud in the earth without right, and for your ungodliness,"' 46.20 (19).

'He once lived among his family joyfully; he surely thought he would never revert,' 84.13,14.

God as judge

God is described in the Qur'an as the supreme and strictly righteous judge:

'Is not God the justest of judges?,' 95.8

He is the judge of judges in the sense that he is the best one to pass judgment, 7.87 (85); cf. 10.109; 12.80.

God can appear as sovereign judge in the last judgment to pronounce judgment, because he is the omnipotent creator of human beings. To those who declare the judgment lies, 82.9, the Qur'an says:

'And what shall teach thee what is the Day of Doom? Again, what shall teach thee what is the Day of Doom? A day when no soul shall possess aught to succour another soul; that day the Command shall belong to God,' 82.17–19; cf. 95.7,8.

The preaching of the last judgment in the Qur'an is very impressive. An idea is given of the catastrophe which will then take place. The hour is said to be near, although only God knows when it will overtake people. This will cause great panic to the sinners and the rich. Cold shivers run down one's back when one hears or reads these texts.

The last judgment begins with a cosmic catastrophe. The terrors which are depicted aim to move hearers to repentance and to make them repent, to compel haste to believe in the message of the prophet and so avoid the judgment that threatens:

> 'Upon the day when man shall remember what he has striven,' 79.35.

That is, when the veils and the coverings are taken away from the eyes, 50.22 (21), and what is in people's hearts is brought to light, 100.10.

Although the judgment affects both communities and their prophets, it is primarily addressed to the individual. The individual will stand before God alone, 19.80 (83). He will get no help from his relatives, friends, clan, tribe or nation:

> 'Now you have come to Us one by one, as We created you upon the first time,' 6.94.

Precisely because of what a person otherwise expects, he is now called on to ponder that what he now does has consequences for tomorrow. One will get to see what one did the day before yesterday, 59.18:

> 'Upon the day (when punishment comes,) when heaven shall be as molten copper and the mountains shall be as plucked wool-tufts, no loyal friend shall question loyal friend, as they are given sight of them (each will be preoccupied with himself). The sinner will wish that he might ransom himself from the chastisement of that day even by his sons, his companion wife, his brother, his kin who sheltered him, and whosoever is in the earth, all together, so that then it might deliver him,' 70.8–14.

> 'There shall not be accepted from any one of them the whole earth full of gold, if he would ransom himself thereby,' 3.91 (85); cf. 5.36 (40); 13.18; 39.47 (48); 10.54 (55).

> 'When earth is shaken with a mighty shaking and earth brings forth her burdens (namely the dead), and Man says, "What ails her?," upon that day she shall tell her tidings for that her Lord has inspired her. Upon that day men shall issue in scatterings to see their works, and whoso has done an atom's weight of good shall see it, and whoso has done an atom's weight of evil shall see it,' 99.1–8.

This last is typical of the Qur'an, which here wants to emphasize that God will be strictly righteous in His judgment. Each will bear his own burden; everyone will see what he has done, whether good or bad:

> '. . . no soul laden bears the load of another,' 17.15 (16); cf. 6.164; 35.38 (19); 39.7 (9); 53.38 (39).

> 'It is decided among them with righteousness and no injustice is done to them,' 10.45.

> 'Are they recompensed in a different way from their deeds?', 10.52 (53).

That is the question, which clearly intends to elicit the response 'No, never.'

Reckoning

Numerous passages of the Qur'an talk about the reckoning, about profit and loss, and about the weighing of deeds. This terminology must be seen against the background of the commercial life of Mecca. C.C.Torrey has spoken in this connection of the commercial-theological language of the Qur'an.

The term 'righteousness' or 'fairness' can also be understood in this way.

This word is also used in the Qur'an in connection with fair standards and the obligations in trading. Numerous admonitions appear in the Qur'an to give full measure and the full weight with righteousness (or justice).

> 'O my people, fill up the measure and the balance justly, and do not diminish the goods of the people,' 11.85 (86).

> 'Woe to the stinters who, when they measure against the people, take full measure (want to have the full pound), but, when they measure for them or weigh for them, do skimp,' 83.1–3.

This terminology is also used in talk about the heavenly accounting and drawing up the balance at the last reckoning.

> 'And We shall set up the just balances for the Resurrection Day, so that not one soul shall be wronged anything; even if it be the weight of one grain of mustard-seed We shall produce it, and sufficient are We for reckoners,' 21.47 (48); cf. 6.152 (153); 7.42 (40).

> 'Every nation has its Messenger; then when their Messenger comes, justly the issue is decided between them, and they are not wronged,' 10.47 (48); cf. 6.160 (161); 23.62 (64).

Description of the last day

Both chapters 81 and 82 give a shocking announcement of the judgment and the verdict that people can expect on that day:

> 'When the sun shall be darkened,
> when the stars shall be thrown down,
> when the mountains shall be set moving,
> when the pregnant camels shall be neglected,
> when the savage beast shall be mustered,
> when the seas shall be set boiling,
> when the souls shall be coupled,
> when the buried infant shall be asked for what sin she was slain,
> when the scrolls (on which the deeds of men are written) shall be unrolled,
> when heaven shall be stripped off,
> when Hell shall be set blazing,
> when Paradise shall be brought nigh,
> then shall a soul know what it has produced,' 81.1–14.

The burial of a girl – when still alive – (mentioned in v.10) presumably refers to the fact that out of poverty, or also because of the negative feelings towards girls in the pre-Islamic period, there was a custom of burying girls alive after their births. According to another translation girls are buried alive in order to promote the fertility of the land. Elsewhere we read in the Qur'an:

> 'And when any of them is given the good tidings of a girl, his face is darkened and he chokes inwardly, as he hides him from the people because of the evil of the good tidings that have been given unto him, *whether he shall preserve it in humiliation, or trample it into the dust.* Ah, evil is that they judge!,' 16.58, 59 (60, 61); cf. 43.17 (16).

The first verses of 82 read:

> 'When the heaven is split open,
> when the stars are scattered,
> when the seas swarm over,
> when the tombs are overthrown,
> then a soul shall know its works, the former and the latter,' 82.1–5.

The judgment: reward or punishment

There is specific mention of reward in the Qur'an in connection with the contrast between the fates awaiting the elect and the damned.

> 'So, when the Trumpet is blown with a single blast and the earth and the mountains are lifted up and crushed with a single blow,

> then, on that day, the Terror shall come to pass,
> and heaven shall be split, for upon that day it shall be very frail,
> and the angels shall stand upon its borders, and upon that day eight shall carry above them the Throne of thy Lord.
>
> On that day you shall be exposed, not one secret of yours concealed. Then as for him who is given his book in his right hand, he shall say, "Here, take and read my book! Certainly I thought that I should encounter my reckoning."
>
> So he shall be in a pleasing life in a lofty Garden, its clusters nigh to gather. "Eat and drink with wholesome appetite for that you did long ago, in the days gone by."
>
> But as for him who is given his book (with his deeds) in his left hand, he shall say, "Would that I had not been given my book and not known my reckoning! Would it had been the end! My wealth has not availed me, my authority is gone from me!"', 69.13–29; cf. further 80.33–42; 84.7–14; 88.1–16; 56.1–56; 78.17–36; 17.71 (73); 45.29. (28).

It is important to note that this reward and punishment are not given equally.

The reward is always abundant, whereas the punishment is stingy:

> 'Whosoever does an evil deed shall be recompensed only with the like of it, but whosoever does a righteous deed, be it male or female, believing – those shall enter Paradise, therein provided without reckoning,' 40.40 (43); cf. 4.123, 124 (122, 123).

> 'Whoso brings a good deed *shall have ten the like of it*;
> and whoso brings an evil deed shall only be recompensed the like of it; they shall not be wronged,' 6.160 (161).

Evil has its consequences, unless it is forgiven and done away with:

> 'Surely God shall not wrong so much as the weight of an ant; and if it be a good deed He will *double* it, and give from Himself a mighty wage,' 4.40 (44).

On the day of judgment not only the (mis)deeds of people will be judged but also their beliefs. Then any remaining uncertainties or lack of clarity will be brought to a decision, on the 'day of decision' which Muhammad's opponents declare to be a lie, 37.21; cf. 44.40; 77.13, 38. The difference with Christians over their understanding of Jesus is also one of the things about which disunity and division exist and which will be resolved:

> '. . . I will decide between you, as to what you were at variance on,' 3.55 (48).

Then God will also judge Jews and Christians who dispute that they can ever prove anything, 2.113 (107). There is also mention of the decision that God will make at the last judgment in connection with Muhammad's opponents in Mecca, 10.93.

Heaven and hell

The destination of the one is heaven, the garden and paradise, and of the other hell and fire:

> 'Then the unbelievers shall be driven in companies into Gehenna till, when they come thither, then its gates will be opened and its keepers will say to them, "Did not Messengers come to you from among yourselves, reciting to you the signs of your Lord and warning you against the encounter of this your day?" They shall say, "Yes indeed; but the word of the chastisement has been realized against the unbelievers." It shall be said, "Enter the gates of Gehenna, to dwell therein forever." How evil is the lodging of those that are proud!
>
> Then those that feared their Lord shall be driven in companies into Paradise, till, when they have come thither, and its gates are opened, and its keepers will say to them, "Peace be upon you! Well you have fared; enter in, to dwell forever." And they shall say, "Praise belongs to God, who has been true in His promise to us, and has bequeathed upon us the earth, for us to make our dwelling wheresoever we will in Paradise. How excellent is the wage of those that labour!,"' 39.71–74.

The descriptions of paradise and hell, of the delights which come as a reward for the deeds done on earth and the punishments and the torment in the fire of hell as retribution for what has been done wrongly or not done at all occupy a very important place in the Qur'an.

As for paradise, there is mention of the garden, 2.111 (105), 214 (210); the garden of Eden, 9.72 (73) etc.; the garden of eternal life, 25.15 (16); the garden of destiny or refuge, 32.19; 53.15; the garden of paradise, 18.107; the high garden, 88.10; the high halls, 25.75; the house of peace (*dar al-salam*) 6.127; 10.25 (26) and the pleasure garden, 30.15 (16). It is the garden through which rivers flow, 2.25 (23) etc.; rivers of wine and honey, 47.15. The food and shade there are everlasting, 13.35. The breadth of paradise is like the breadth of both heaven and earth, 57.21; 3.133 (127). Life in paradise is described in concrete detail, above all in the preaching of the first period in Mecca. People are richly provided with fruit and meat, to their heart's desire, 52.22, and they will be offered wine to drink:

> 'In the Gardens of Bliss upon couches, set face to face, a cup from a spring being passed round to them, white, a delight to the drinkers, wherein no sickness is, neither intoxication,' 37.43–47 (42–46).

The elect will delight in the company of their parents, their spouses and children who are believers, 13.23; 36.56; 40.8. They will praise their Lord who has taken away their sorrow, 35.34 (31). The anger that was in their hearts is taken away, 15.47. They are like brothers, 15.47; and they will turn to one another to question one another, 52.25:

> 'And those that believe, and do deeds of righteousness, them We shall admit to gardens underneath which rivers flow, therein dwelling forever and ever; therein for them shall be spouses purified, and We shall admit them to a shelter of plenteous shade,' 4.57 (60).

For them, what they want is there and still more, 50.35 (34); cf. 10.26 (27):

> 'Surely the godfearing shall be in gardens and (in a state of) bliss, rejoicing in that their Lord has given them; and their Lord shall guard them against the chastisement of Hell. "Eat and drink, with wholesome appetite, for that you were working." Reclining upon couches ranged in rows; and We shall espouse them to wide-eyed houris, and those who believed, and their seed followed them in belief. We shall join their seed with them, and We shall not defraud them of aught of their work; every man shall be pledged for what he earned.
>
> And We shall succour them with fruits and flesh such as they desire while they pass therein a cup one to another wherein is no idle talk, no cause of sin, and there go round them youths, their own, as if they were hidden pearls. They advance one upon another, asking each other questions. They say, "We were before among our people, ever going in fear, and God was gracious to us, and guarded us against the chastisement of the burning wind,"' 52.17–27.

It is often pointed out that the notions of paradise in the Qur'an are very concrete and have a sensual colouring, like an oasis for men, 44.54; 56.22; 55.72; 37.48 (47).

This notion is to some degree kept in balance by the following verse:

> 'God has promised the believers, men, gardens underneath which rivers flow, forever therein to dwell, and goodly dwelling-places in the Gardens of Eden; *and greater, God's good pleasure; that is the mighty triumph*,' 9.72 (73).

The descriptions of hell which are given in the Qur'an do not mince words. There is mention of hell (*jahannam*), 2.206 (202); the fire of hell, 31.21 (20); the heat of hell, 74.27; hell-fire, 26.91; or just fire 90.20; glowing fire, 33.64; and blazing fire, 101.11. The fire is said to be impenetrable, 90.20; a fire that flames up, 92.14; and that rises above the human heart, 104.6. For the wicked, fire means moaning and groaning, 11.106 (108).

The evildoers are punished in hell, 7.41.

The fiery glow is prepared for those who declare the Hour to be a lie, 25.11 (12). The hypocrites are in hell-fire, 82.14. *jahannam* or hell is the destination of unbelievers.

Fire is prepared for the unbelievers; people and stones (of idols) form the fuel, 2.24 (22). The fiery *glow* is prepared for the unbelievers, 48.13. The unbelievers will die alive in the fire, 87.13; cf. 20.74 (76). It is said of a rich young man that he will burn in the heat of hell, 74.26. There is talk of scorching in hell-fire, 69.31; of the heat of hell, 74.26; of the glow of hell, 84.12. Those who are there have neither coolness nor drink, 78.24:

> 'They also say, "If we had only heard, or had understood,
> we would not have been of the inhabitants of the Blaze,"' 67.10.

There is a prayer in the Qur'an in which asks for protection from hell fire:

> '. . . forgive those who have repented, and follow Thy way, and guard them against the chastisement of Hell,' 40.7; cf. 44.45.

But the Qur'an says that there are no helpers in the fire, 29.25 (24):

> '. . . shalt thou deliver him out of the Fire?,' 39.19 (20).

As in Matthew 25.31, which talks about the sheep and the goats who stand at the left and right before the king at the last judgment, so too the Qur'an speaks of people on the right hand and on the left. The people on the left side have the opposite qualities to those of 'the companions of paradise'. The unbelievers form a long procession and march to hell. From the description it becomes clear how these people have got into such company.

Among those who take part in the procession are people who declare God a liar, 56.51–56; 52.9–16; the evildoers, 37.62–68 (60–66); the defiant, 40.60 (62); the unashamed, 78.21–26; those who neglect the commandments of God or the rules of moral behaviour, 82.13–16; those who depart from the right course, 72.14,15; those who rebel against God and his emissary, 72.23 (24); the hypocrites, 66.9; those who mock revelation, 18.106; those who express suspicions, 51.10–14 and finally those who have no faith, never do social work on behalf of the poor or the old, 50.24–26 (23–25). The Qur'an also mentions liars;

people who only swear wildly; people who abstain from the good; transgressors; and people who have rough manners, 68.8–16. According to the Qur'an people who end up in hell themselves say:

> 'We were not of those who prayed,
> and we fed not the needy, and we plunged along with the plungers, and we cried lies to the Day of Doom, till the Certain came to us (i.e. death overcame us),' 74.43–47 (44–48).

Really four actions stand out which lead most to punishment in hell:

1. Not performing prayer (*salat*).
2. Not giving to the needy (*zakat*).
3. Idle talk about religious things
4. Declaring God and his Hour a lie.

On the other side there is a summary of the conditions which must be met if one wants to belong to those who are admitted into the heavenly gardens.

The reward of paradise is promised only to the worshippers who persist in prayer and who regard the good; a recognized part of whose wealth is for the beggar and those without possessions; who believe that the day of judgment is true; who fear the punishment of their Lord; who preserve their shame; who bear witness and respect their obligations in prayer (70.22–34).

> '[Those] who fulfil God's covenant, and break not the compact, who join what God has commanded shall be joined, and fear their Lord, and dread the evil reckoning, patient men, desirous of the Face of their Lord, who perform the prayer, and expend of that We have provided them, secretly and in public, and who avert evil with good – theirs shall be the Ultimate Abode, Gardens of Eden which they shall enter,' 13.20–23.

Passages to look up

In various places in the Qur'an there is mention of the cities and the verdict that is spoken on them, 47.13 (14).

If only they had believed but they did not, 7.96–101 (94–99). An ungrateful city is presented as a warning example, 16.112, 113 (113,114); cf. also the passage about the traveller who passes a fallen city, 2.259 (261). Also the story of an unnamed city (Antioch), 36.13–29 (12–28). Many cities are overwhelmed because of unbelief, 11.100–102 (102–104). That does nto happen if their inhabitants do good, 11.117 (119). Such a fate does not befall them unless a messenger is sent to them, 28.59; cf. 26.208, or they are in possession of a book, 15.4.

6

God's Power and Human Responsibility

'Alike is it to them whether thou has warned them or thou hast not warned them, they do not believe,' 36.10 (9).

'No compulsion is there in religion,' 2.256 (257).

'God changes not what is in a people, until they change what is in themselves,' 13.11 (12).

Introduction

The impression is often given that the Qur'an emphasizes the power of God so strongly that there is no longer any room for human beings to make their own free decision. Is the God of the Qur'an a kind of Fate or a capricious judge? Does He not have the fate of men in His hands to such a degree that everything is already determined in advance? That is the impression which often not only non-Muslims but also Muslims themselves give of the Qur'anic image of God.

The fact that the Qur'an explicitly speaks of reward according to works – what people have or have not done – points in a different direction from fatalism. In the Qur'an people are called on to take the right way and not to wander from it. Certainly it is often said of God that he leads on the right way as He wills and on a false way as He wills. There is even talk of God sealing hearts. Can we then speak of what is popularly called *qadar* or *taqdir*, predestination to evil, as well? However much God may determine things, it is made clear that God does not do injustice to anyone. According to the Qur'an people do injustice to themselves. The way to forgiveness stands open and clearly breaks through the notion of a rigid doctrine of predestination.

Reward for works

In certain places in the Qur'an it clearly emerges that people themselves are responsible for the evil deeds that they do.

> 'And if a good thing visits them, they say, "This is from God"; but if an evil thing visits them, they say, "This is from thee,"' 4.79 (81); cf. 42.30 (29); 3.165 (159).

In Muhammad's earliest preaching, where the announcement of the last judgment comes more into the foreground than it does later, it is indicated that the punishment affects those who declare the last judgment a lie and turn from it, while the godfearers will escape judgment, 92.16,17; cf. 107. There are numerous passages in the Qur'an which emphasize *recompense according to works* and the strict righteousness of the judgment:

> 'Today each soul shall be recompensed for that it has earned; no wrong today. Surely God is swift at the reckoning,' 40.17; cf. 2.202 (198).
>
> '... whoso has done an atom's weight of good shall see it, and whoso has done an atom's weight of evil shall see it,' 99.7,8.
>
> '... and every soul shall be paid in full what it has earned, and they shall not be wronged,' 3.25 (24).

Nothing happens to human beings other than what they have brought upon themselves, and one day what they have done will be seen, 53.38–40 (39–41). No one is given another's burden to carry, 53.58 (39); cf. 6.164; 17.15; 35.18; 39.7.

The Qur'an repeatedly emphasizes that every man individually and every people collectively are responsible for what they do:

> 'The unbelievers say to the believers, "Follow our path, and let us carry your offences"; yet they cannot carry anything, even of their own offences; they are truly liars. They shall certainly carry their loads, and other loads along with their loads, and upon the Day of Resurrection they shall surely be questioned concerning that they were forging,' 29.12 ,13 (11, 12).

Then the Qur'an speaks of God who guides people in a particular direction:

> 'As for him who gives and is godfearing and confirms the reward most fair, We shall surely ease him to the Easing.
>
> But as for him who is a miser, and self-sufficient, and cries lies to the reward most fair, We shall surely ease him to the Hardship,' 92.5–10; cf. 87.7.

Going on the right way and departing from it

The imagery which is often used in the Qur'an is that of the *way, the right way* on which a person is guided or from which he departs. The main image must be that of the wilderness, where wandering from the way, losing direction, is fatal. Finding or losing the way in the desert is literally a question of life or death. Therefore it is of vital importance to have a guide and to get the right guidance:

> 'When we heard the guidance, we believed in it; and whosoever believes in his Lord, he shall fear neither paltriness nor vileness. And some of us have surrendered, and some of us have deviated. Those who have surrendered sought rectitude,' 72.13,14.

> '. . . and surely they that believe not in the world to come are deviating from the path,' 23.74 (76).

The characteristic of God's way is that it is 'right'. The way that God shows through his instructions and signs is the right way. If you take it, walk on it or follow it, you arrive at the destination. As God says in the Qur'an:

> 'And that this is My path, straight; so do you follow it, and follow not divers paths lest they scatter you from His path,' 6.153 (154); cf. 6.126.

The unbelievers are those who are constantly occupied in making God's straight way crooked.

> '. . . why do you bar from God's way the believer, desiring to make it crooked?,' 3.99 (94).

> 'Then a herald shall proclaim between them: "God's curse is on the evildoers who bar from God's way, desiring to make it crooked, disbelieving in the world to come,"' 7.44, 45 (42, 43).

Error

The opposite to right guidance is error, losing the way, wandering. Those who have kept the scripture hidden:

> 'Those are they that have bought error at the price of guidance, and chastisement at the price of pardon,' 2.175 (170).

The time for the coming of the revelation, often called the time of ignorance, is also characterized as the time of error. It is even said of Muhammad in the Qur'an that he was first in error:

> 'Did He (God) not find thee (Muhammad) erring, and guide thee?,' 93.7.

There is even more talk of error that one has deliberately chosen – and how evil it is: according to the Qur'an there are people who know the right way but do not take it, indeed who even choose to take the wrong way, 7.146 (143):

> 'Surely those who disbelieve, and bar from the way of God, have gone astray into far error,' 4.167 (165).

The Qur'an says that following one's own inclinations and desires is the cause of error:

> 'Say: "I (Muhammad) do not follow your caprices, or else I had gone astray, and would not be of the right-guided,"' 6.56.
>
> '. . . who is further astray than he who follows his caprice without guidance from God?,' 28.50.
>
> '[Abraham said]: "If my Lord does not guide me
> I shall surely be of the people gone astray,"' 6.77.

Over against desire and one's own inclination stands 'knowledge' as this has been revealed:

> 'If thou followest their caprices, after the knowledge that has come to thee, then thou wilt surely be among the evildoers,' 2.145 (140).

Does God make people err?

> 'Nay, but the evildoers follow their own caprices, without knowledge; so who shall guide those whom God has led astray? They have no helpers,' 30.29 (28).
>
> 'And those who cry lies to Our signs are deaf and dumb, dwelling in the shadows (have gone astray). Whomsoever God will, He leads astray, and whomsoever He will, He sets him on a straight path,' 6.39.
>
> 'Whomsoever God desires to guide, He expands his breast to Islam; whomsoever He desires to lead astray, He makes his breast narrow, tight, as if he were climbing to heaven. So God lays abomination upon those who believe not,' 6.125.
>
> 'Whomsoever God guides, he is rightly guided; and whom He leads astray – thou wilt not find for them protectors,' 17.97.cf. 18.17 (16).
>
> 'Whomsoever God leads astray, no guide he has; He leaves them in their insolence blindly wandering,' 7.186 (185); cf. 13.33.

> 'We have sent no Messenger save with the tongue of his people, that he might make all clear to them; then God leads astray whomsoever He will, and He guides whomsoever He will; and He is the All-mighty, the All-wise,' 14.4; cf. 35.8 (9); 74.31,34.

> 'The unbelievers say, "Why has a sign not been sent down upon him from his Lord?" Say: "God leads astray whomsoever He will, and He guides to Him all who are penitent,"' 13.27.

> 'The unbelievers say, "Why has a sign not been sent down upon him from his Lord?" Thou art only a warner, and a guide to every people,' 13.7 (8); cf. 10.20 (21); 6.37.

The Qur'an itself goes so far as to assert:

> 'If God had willed, He would have made you one nation; but He leads astray whom He will, and guides whom He will; and you will surely be questioned about the things you wrought,' 16.93 (95); cf. 11.118 (10); 42.8 (6).

> 'If We had so willed, We could have given every soul its guidance; but now My Word is realized – "Assuredly I shall fill Gehenna with *jinns* and men all together"', 32.13; cf. 11.119 (120).

On the other hand it is also true that:

> 'But whomso God guides, none shall lead him astray,' 39.37 (38).

However, the last series of images seems to indicate that God, as is repeatedly said, guides on the right way those whom he wills and on the wrong way those whom he wills. If he does this, and above all also makes people err, is man then still responsible and free?

Muhammad can compel no one to faith

The Qur'an asserts that Muhammad himself cannot guide people rightly. God guides rightly those whom He wills, 28.56. He leads whom He wills to his light, 24.35.

It is made clear to Muhammad that it is not in his power and capacity to convert people. His task is to warn, to remind and to preach:

> '. . . thou art not charged to oversee them,' 88.22; cf. 6.107. He cannot compel them, 50.45 (44).

The thought of compulsion is rejected:

> 'And if thy Lord had willed, whoever is in the earth would have

believed, all of them, all together. Wouldst thou then constrain the people, until they are believers?,' 10.99.

'Thou canst not make those in their tombs to hear,' 35.22 (21); cf. 11.12 (15); 88.22; 5.92 (93), 99; 88.22; 21.45 (46); 30.52 (51).

'And if their turning away is distressful for thee, why, if thou canst seek out a hole in the earth (if you want to sink into the ground), or a ladder in heaven, to bring them some sign (you should do so, is the thought that is not expressed further), but had God willed, he would have gathered them to the guidance,' 6.35.

'Thou shalt not make the dead to hear, neither shalt thou make the deaf to hear the call when they turn about, retreating. Thou shalt not guide the blind out of their error neither shalt thou make any to hear, save such as believe in Our signs, and so surrender,' 27.80, 81 (82, 83).

'And some of them give ear to thee; what, wilt thou make the deaf to hear, though they understand not? And some of them look unto thee; what, wilt thou then guide the blind, though they do not see?,' 10.42, 43 (43, 44); cf. 30.52 (51).

'Or deemest thou (Muhammad) that most of them hear or understand? they are but as the cattle; nay, they are further astray from the way,' 25.44 (46).

God seals hearts

There are a few statements in the Qur'an which are even more explicit about God's activity in making people err, namely those which speak about sealing the heart or placing a veil:

'Surely We have laid veils on their hearts lest they understand it, and in their ears heaviness; and though thou callest them to the guidance, yet they will not be guided ever,' 18.57 (55).

'And some of them there are that listen to thee, and We lay veils upon their hearts lest they understand it, and in their ears heaviness; and if they see any sign whatever, they do not believe in it (the Qur'an), so that when they come to thee they dispute with thee, the unbelievers saying, "This is naught but the fairy-tales of the ancient ones,"' 6.25; cf. 17.46 (48).

'Hast thou seen him who has taken his caprice to be his god, and God has led him astray out of a knowledge, and set a seal upon his hearing and his heart, and laid a covering on his eyes? Who shall guide him after God? What, will you not remember?,' 45.23 (22); cf. 25.43 (45).

Whom does God then guide rightly and whom does He make to err?

The Qur'an says that God guides on the right way those who listen; who are upright and fear God. He does not guide the unrighteous and He does not guide the transgressors. God does not guide those who do injustice, 2.258 (260); 9.109 (110); 46.10 (9); 6.144 (145); He does not guide the unbelieving, 2.264 (266), 9.19–37; 16.107 (109); nor those who do evil, 5.108 (107); 9.80 (81); 61.5,7; 62.5; 63.6.

Talking about the meaning of a parable (the gnat), the Qur'an says:

'Thereby He leads many astray, and thereby He guides many; and thereby He leads none astray *save the ungodly*,' 2.26 (24).

'How shall God guide a people who have disbelieved after they believed, and bore witness that the Messenger is true, and the clear signs came to them? God guides not the people of the evildoers,' 3.86 (80).

'People of the Book, now there has come to you Our Messenger, making clear to you many things you have been concealing of the Book, and effacing many things. There has come to you from God a light, and a Book Manifest whereby God guides *whosoever follows His good pleasure* in the ways of peace, and brings them forth from the shadows into the light by His leave; and He guides them to a straight path,' 5.15, 16 (18).

'God chooses unto Himself whomsoever He will, and He guides to Himself *whosoever turns, penitent*,' 42.13 (12).

It is impossible to bring the different texts in the Qur'an and the statements that they contain under one heading and make a harmonious whole of them. The Qur'an is not a dogmatic treatise. Muhammad was a prophet, not a theologian.

On the one hand these verses indicate that God makes people deaf and blind and seals or veils the hearts, but on the other the passages end – in 45.23 (22) – with a call to be admonished. Something of the same thing can be said about the preaching of judgment and the threat of punishment. The point is for people to convert in time and to turn away from such dangerous possibilities that they might otherwise expect:

'Surely the evildoers are friends one of the other; God is the friend of the godfearing,' 45.19 (18).

Responsibility for evil comes before human reckoning, while the good is owed to God:

> 'And if a good thing visits them, they say, "This is from God"; but if an evil thing visits them, they say, "This is from thee,"' 4.79 (81).

Asking for forgiveness

However often the Qur'an may talk of God's power and God's will, people are called on to worship God and are assured that God hears their prayers.

> 'Your Lord has said, "Call upon Me and I will answer you,"'40.60 (62); 2.186 (182); 11.61 (64); 27.62 (63); 6.41.

When the Qur'an says:

> 'God charges no soul save to its capacity; standing to its account is what it has earned, and against its account what it has merited,' 2.286; cf. 2.253; 6.152 (153); 7.42 (40); 23.63 (64),

these words are followed in the same verse by a prayer:

> 'Our Lord, take us not to task if we forget, or make mistake.
> Our Lord, charge us not with a load such as Thou didst lay upon those before us.
> Our Lord, do Thou not burden us beyond what we have the strength to bear.
> And pardon us, and forgive us, and have mercy on us;
> Thou art our Protector. And help us against the people of the unbelievers,' 2.286.

The Qur'an calls on people to ask God for forgiveness, 11.3; 71.10 (9); 73.20; 110.3:

> 'And say: "My Lord, forgive and have mercy, for Thou art the best of the merciful,"' 23.118.

> 'Race to forgiveness from your lord,' 57.21.

Those who ask God for forgiveness will receive it:

> 'Whosoever does evil, or wrongs himself, and then prays God's forgiveness, he shall find God is All-forgiving, All-compassionate,' 4.110; cf. 3.135 (129); 4.64 (67).

Therefore people must not despair of God's forgiveness, 39.53 (54). God may wipe out the evil that believers have committed, 39.35 (36):

> 'Our Lord, forgive Thou us our sins and acquit us of our evil deeds,

and take us to Thee with the pious,' 3.193 (191); 3.16 (14); 3.147 (141).

'We believe in our Lord, that He may pardon us our offences,' 20.78.

'We are eager that our Lord should forgive us our offences, for that we are the first of the believers', 26.51.

'There is a party of My servants who said, "Our Lord, we believe; therefore forgive us, and have mercy on us, for Thou art the best of the merciful,"' 23.109 (111).

It is said that Muhammad found no hearing when he attempted to convert the people of Ta'if, a city east of Mecca. But the *jinns* did listen to him. These *jinns* then say:

'O our people, answer God's summoner, and believe in Him, and He will forgive you some of your sins, and protect you from a painful chastisement,' 46.31 (30).

Thus God is described in the Qur'an as the one who forgives:

'Yet I am All-forgiving to him who repents and believes, and does righteousness, and at last is guided,' 20.82 (84).

While Satan promises poverty and incites to immorality, God promises forgiveness, 2.268 (271); cf. 2.169 (164); 2.284.

God forgives those whom He wills and punishes those whom He wills, 48.14. Verses of the Qur'an repeatedly end with expressions like 'God is forgiving' or even in a stronger form, 'loves to forgive', 48.14; 24.22; 38.66; 39.53 (54); 40.42 (45); 71. 10 (9); 73.20.

It is said of God that He forgives everything, 42.30 (20), 34 (32). Forgiveness belongs to Him, 74.56:

'If you do good openly or in secret or pardon an evil, surely God is All-pardoning, All-powerful,' 4.149 (148).

'And those who believe, and do righteous deeds, We shall surely acquit them of their evil deeds, and shall recompense them the best of what they were doing,' 29.7 (6).

The Qur'an also contains the encouragement to forgive others with the motivation:

'Do you not wish that God should forgive you?,' 24.22.

According to the Qur'an, for what sins can forgiveness be asked?

Among the great sins the Qur'an understands: killing one's own children for fear of poverty, fornication, deliberate murder, stealing the property of the orphan, dishonesty in trade, immodesty and arrogance, 17.31–37 (33–39). God has forbidden immorality, open or secret sin and illegitimate desires, 7.33 (31). Open and hidden sins must be given up, 6.120. The Qur'an says that anyone who refrains from such great sins will be forgiven.

God will take away the evil deeds and admit him to paradise, 4.31 (35):

> 'Those who avoid the heinous sins and indecencies, save lesser offences – surely thy Lord is wide in His forgiveness,' 53.32 (33); cf. 42.37 (35).

However, there is one sin which is not forgiven, namely giving God a consort/partner/companion. Here of course one must think of polytheism, giving a place to the idols of Muhammad's time: Al-Lat, Al-'Uzza, Manat or Hobal, alongside God. But it also refers to any idol to whom is given the loyalty that belongs to God alone. Such an idol can be one's own desires:

> 'Hast thou seen him who has taken his caprice to be his god? Wilt thou be a guardian over them?,' 25.43 (45); cf. 45.23 (22).

> 'God forgives not that aught should be with Him associated; less than that He forgives to whomsoever he will,' 4.48 (51); cf. 4.116.

The prophet Muhammad and believers may not ask for forgiveness for polytheists, even if they are relatives, as soon as it has become clear that they are people from hell, 9.113 (114). In this connection Abraham is cited as an example who asked for forgiveness for his father, 9.114 (115); cf. 19.47 (48); 26.86; 60.4; 14.41. It is also said of Noah that he prayed:

> 'My Lord, forgive me and my parents and whosoever enters my house as a believer, and the believers, men and women alike,' 7.28 (29); cf. 11.41 (43), 45, 46 (47, 48).

But the prayer for his son was rejected, 11.45, 46 (47, 48).

Repentance

In the Qur'an people are called on to convert or repent. From the human side *taba* (the word used here) means 'convert'; from God's side *taba* means forgiveness.

Repentance is accepted by God:

> 'But whoso repents, after his evildoing, and makes amends, God will turn towards him; God is All-forgiving, All-compassionate,' 5.39 (43).

He accepts repentance from whom He wills, 9.15; cf. 9.27. He accepts the repentance of *His servants*, 9.104 (105):

> 'It is He who accepts repentance from His servants, and pardons evil deeds; He knows the things you do,' 42.25 (24).

> 'Believers, turn to God in sincere repentance; it may be that your Lord will acquit you of your evil deeds, and will admit you into gardens underneath which rivers flow,' 66.8.

It is possible that God will accept the repentance of those who recognize their wickedness, 9.102 (103):

> '. . . save him who repents, and believes, and does righteous work – those, God will change their evil deeds into good deeds, for God is ever All-forgiving, All-compassionate,' 25.70.

Of the 'people of Moses' who worship the golden calf it is said:

> 'Surely those who took to themselves the Calf (cf. the golden calf in Exodus 32) – anger shall overtake them from their Lord, and abasement in this present life; so We recompense those who are forgers. And those who do evil deeds, then repent thereafter and believe, surely thereafter thy Lord is All-forgiving, All-compassionate,' 7.152, 153; cf. 2.54 (51).

When Pharaoh asks for forgiveness shortly before his death, his appeal seems to be rejected:

> 'When the drowning overtook him he (the Pharaoh who persecuted the Israelites) said:
> "I believe that there is no god but He in whom the Children of Israel believe; I am of those that surrender." "Now? And before thou didst rebel, being of those that did corruption. So today We shall deliver thee with thy body, that thou mayest be a sign to those after thee. Surely many men are heedless of Our signs,"' 10.90–92.

This could possibly imply that while his body is saved (corpses were so important that they were embalmed in ancient Egypt), his conversion or repentance are not accepted.

God is prepared to accept the repentance of those who have committed evil unthinkingly and repented promptly. For those who permanently do evil, repentance is not accepted:

> 'God shall turn only towards those who do evil in ignorance, then shortly repent; God will return towards those; God is All-knowing, All-wise.
>
> But God shall not turn towards those who do evil deeds until, when one of them is visited by death, he says, "Indeed now I repent," neither to those who die disbelieving; for them We have prepared a painful chastisement,' 4.17,18 (21, 22)

Muslims often say *maktub*, 'it is written', to indicate that everything is in God's hands. It is therefore appropriate finally to point out that in using this verb the Qur'an says that God has shown mercy:

> 'Your Lord has prescribed for Himself mercy (*kutiba*). Whosoever of you does evil in ignorance, and thereafter repents and makes amends, He is All-forgiving, All-compassionate,' 6.54; cf. 6.12; 16.119 (10); 24.5; 25.71.

Passages to look up

Different words are used in the Qur'an to denote 'sin'. It was impossible in the survey above always to mention the basic Arab words. Finally, to get an impression of these different terms and the contexts in which they are used, here are a few references that can be investigated. As will be noted, the translations of these words are not always identical.

For 'sin', in Arabic *dhanb* (plural *dhunub*): 3.11 (9); 16 (14); 31 (29), 135 (129), 147 (149), 193 (191); 7.100 (98); 9.102 (103); 12.29; 14.10; 25.58 (60); 33.71; 40.3 (2), 11 (14), 21 (22), 55 (57); 46.31(30); 47.19 (21); 48.2; 71.4; 91.14.

'Great sins', in Arabic *kaba'ir*: 4.31(35); 42.37(35); 53.32 (33).

'False step', in Arabic *khata* (plural *akhata*), and further derivations of the word (those who take such a false step): 2.58 (55), 286; 4.92 (94),112; 7.161; 12.29, 91, 97; 17.31(33); 20.73: 26.51, 82; 28.8 (7); 29.12 (11); 33.5; 69.9, 37; 96.16.

'Sinfulness', 'misdeeds', in Arabic *ithm*: 21.85 (79),181(177), 182 (173), 188 (184), 203 (199), 283; 3.178 (173); 4.20 (24), 48 (51), 50 (53), 111,112; 5.2 (3), 29 (32), 62 (67), 63 (68), 106 (105), 107 (106); 6.120; 7.33 (31); 24.11; 3.58; 42.37 (35); 49.12; 53.32(33); 58.8 (9), 9 (10), 76.24.

The Qur'an repeatedly emphasizes that God does no one an injustice: 8.51 (53), 22.10; 3.182 (178), 4.40 (44), 49 (52), 6.131; 50.29 (28); 30.9 (8), 16.118 (119); 11.101(103); 43.76, 16, 33 (35); 3.117 (113); 10.44 (45); 65.1; 2.2, 54 (51), 57 (54), 231; 27.44 (45); 28.161 (15); 7.23 (22), 160, 177 (176), but that people do themselves injustice, 29.50 (39); 2.281.

7

Prophets in General and Abraham in Particular

'We know indeed that it grieves thee the things they say; yet it is not thee they cry lies to, but the evildoers – it is the signs of God that they deny. Messengers indeed were cried lies to before thee, yet they endured patiently that they were cried lies to, and were hurt, until Our help came unto them. No man can change the words of God; and there has already come to thee some tiding of the Envoys,' 6.33, 34.

Introduction

This chapter will discuss the stories of the prophets in the Qur'an, The notion that Muhammad got these stories from informants rather than from God is rejected by the Qur'an. A series of biblical and Arab prophets is mentioned, and the difference between a prophet and envoy or messenger is touched on. The idea is that all have received the same message and all are supported by God and are helped to victory over their opponents. The so-called punishment legends talk of the penalties which peoples who are disobedient will incur. In many stories there seems to be a kind of pattern or scheme in which Muhammad's own experiences served as a model.

Abraham has a special position in these stories, as of course do Adam and above all Moses and Jesus (who will be discussed elsewhere). It is often said of him that he was not a Christian or a Jew but a Muslim. According to the Qur'an Abraham is a model for believers, but that is also said of Muhammad. But only Muhammad is called the seal, the conclusion of the series of prophets.

Borrowing?

In one way or another Muhammad will have learned the biblical stories from Jews and Christians by oral tradition. But the Qur'an rejects the notion that he took them from these or other informants. That is evident from the discussion with his Meccan opponents:

'The unbelievers say, "This is naught but a calumny he has forged, and other folk have helped him to it." . . .

They say, "Fairy-tales of the ancients that he has had written down, so that they are recited to him at the dawn and in the evening."
Say: "He sent it (namely, the revelation) down, who knows the secret in the heavens and earth,"' 25.4–6 (5–7).

'And we know very well that they (the unbelievers) say, "Only a mortal is teaching him." The speech of him at whom they hint is barbarous; and this is speech Arabic, manifest,' 16.103 (105).

For the Qur'an this last is a proof that the revelation which Muhammad receives is not plagiarism or borrowed from the possible informants he might have had.

Prophet and envoy

By prophet (*nabi*) is understood someone who brings news of God. He comes on the one hand to warn people against evil and on the other hand to bring good news. An envoy or messenger (*rasul*) is sent by God to humankind.

The traditional Muslim commentaries make the following distinction: the prophet (*nabi*) is a divine envoy without a law (*shari'a*) and probably without a book, whereas the messenger (*rasul*) comes with one. But such a sharp distinction is difficult to maintain. Sometimes the Qur'an gives religious figures both names, prophet (*nabi*) and messenger (*rasul*): for example Moses, 7.158; 19.52 and Ishmael, 19.54 (55).

The envoy seems rather more important than the prophet. The prophet can be a help to an envoy, as Aaron is to Moses, 19.51, 53 (52, 54).

On the one hand no distinction is made between the messengers. In the catalogue of Abraham, Ishmael, Isaac and Jacob and the patriarchs, Moses and Jesus and the prophets in general, it is said that no distinction is made between them, 2.136 (130), 285; cf. 3.84 (78). But on the other hand it is also said that the messengers are not alike. The one stands above the other, the one is given grace by God or favoured above the other, 2.253 (254); 17.55 (57). In the first instance Jesus is then mentioned as one to whom clear signs are given and who is strengthened with the spirit of holiness, 21.253 (254). In the last case David is mentioned, to whom a scripture (the psalms are meant) is given, 17.55 (57). In this connection one could also think of Moses, the only one to whom God speaks directly, 4.164 (162).

The stories of the prophets in the Qur'an are about the 'biblical' prophets like Noah, Abraham, Moses and Jesus, in other words figures who in the Bible are not always primarily known as prophets. The so-called 'greater' and 'minor' prophets in the Bible, like Isaiah and Jeremiah, are all missing from the Qur'an except for Jonah. Perhaps there is an allusion in the Qur'an to the prophet Ezekiel, 2.259 (261). Alongside this are the stories of the prophets who are not known from the Bible: Sju'ayb who is sent to Midian, Salih who is sent to the tribe of Thamud, and Hud who is sent to the tribe of 'Ad.

Above all chapters 7 and 11 of the Qur'an give more or less systematic accounts of the prophets. However, no 'complete' stories about the prophets are told, but an evocative description is given of particular aspects of their preaching and their activity.

In the following passage a number of 'prophets' are summed up whom Muhammad sees as his predecessors:

> 'And We gave to him Isaac and Jacob – each one We guided. And Noah We guided before; and of his seed David and Solomon, Job and Joseph, Moses and Aaron – even so We recompense the good-doers.
>
> Zechariah and John, Jesus and Elijah; each was of the righteous; Ishmael and Elisha, Jonah and Lot; each one We preferred above all beings;
>
> And of their fathers, and of their seed, and of their brethren; and We elected them, and We guided them to a straight path. That is God's guidance; He guides by it whom He will of His servant; had they been idolaters, it would have failed them, the things they did. Those are they to whom We gave the Book, the Judgment, the Prophethood; so if these disbelieve in it, We have already entrusted it to a people who do not disbelieve in it,' 6.84–89.

> 'We sent Messengers before thee (Muhammad); of some We have related to thee, and some We have not related to thee. It was not for any Messenger to bring a sign, save by God's leave,' 40.78; cf. 4.164 (162).

These prophets or messengers are sent to their peoples, but their message does not have just a local relevance. It has a universal scope.

The Qur'an often speaks of a confrontation on the day of judgment between the prophets and their people, 7.7 (6).

From every community a witness, that is to say a prophet, was sent to them, 16.84 (86); 89 (91); 28.75:

> 'The Messenger (namely, Muhammad) says, "O my Lord, behold, my people have taken this Qur'an as a thing to be shunned,"' 25.30 (32).

Of the series of prophets listed in the Qur'an, Muhammad is seen as the last, as 'the seal', 33.40.

The same message

The Qur'an clearly expresses the notion that in essence all the prophets brought the same message.

God is one and God alone, who alone deserves service and worship (*'ibada*). He alone must be loved and feared. All others are false gods. All the rest is God's servant (*'abd*) and necessarily stands under his command.

Muhammad is convinced of the identity of his message with that of former prophets. He speaks of the identity of the message of all the prophets. All the writings go back to one single source, the heavenly archetype. In the Qur'an this is called the 'mother of the book', 13.39; 43.4 (3), 3.7 (5) or 'the hidden book', 56.78. This means that there must be belief in all the revealed books:

> 'And say: "I (Muhammad) believe in whatever Book God has sent down,"' 42.13.

> 'Surely this is in the ancient scrolls (writings containing revelation), the scrolls of Abraham and Moses,' 87.18,19.

'Book' or writing' often denotes not a particular book but the totality of divine revelations, 2.213 (209).

The notion that all prophets give the same message can even lead to Muslims being recommended in case of doubt to ask the advice of people of the book (that means Jews or Christians):

> 'So, if thou art in doubt regarding what We have sent down to thee, ask those who recited the Book before thee,' 10.94.

Because Muhammad and his followers believe in all the books, however, Muhammad expects that all other communities will believe in the Qur'an, especially communities of Jews and Christians.

The specific feature of the last revelation, the Qur'an, is that it has been revealed in clear Arabic, 16.103 (105); 26.195; 39.28 (29); 41.3 (2); 26.195.

Muhammad certainly sees himself as the one who comes with a clear sign to the adherents of former revelations as well; this clear sign is the Qur'an, which can give enlightenment. The Qur'an can restore the meaning of former books of revelation which have been distorted. Sometimes adherents of former books/scrolls/revelations (or whatever they are called) have expounded the books wrongly:

> 'The unbelievers of the People of the Book and the idolaters would never leave off, till the Clear Sign came to them, a Messenger from God, reciting pages purified, therein true Books,' 98.1, 2, 3.

In the Qur'an it is said that a group of Jews in Medina heard the words of God but then, because they did not know better, distorted them, 2.75 (70). A woe is pronounced on those who write scripture with their own hand and thus falsify it, 2.79 (73) or who take words out of their place, 5.13 (16), 41 (45). This last remark could indicate not just a distortion of the meaning but even a corruption of the text. Another passage in the Qur'an in which it is said that they – again the Jews – twist their tongues in reading from scripture so that it is wrongly thought that what they say is part of scripture, 3.78 (72), may also point in this direction; cf. also 4.46 (48). This notion of the distortion of the meaning of the text or the text itself (about which the Muslims too thought differently later) becomes an argument which can explain why Jews and Christians do not accept Muhammad's message although it is the same. The explanation is that they have corrupted scripture themselves (see also chapter 11 below).

Success

According to the Qur'an divine help and final victory belong to God's messengers and those who help them:

> 'Surely We shall help Our Messengers and those who have believed, in the present life, and upon the day when the witnesses arise,' 40.51 (54).

In chapter 21, which is devoted to the former prophets, one prophet after another is named and his strengthening by God is described.

Of Noah it is said:

> '. . . We helped him against the people who cried lies to Our signs,' 21.77.

Of Moses, Aaron and their successors it is said:

> '. . . We helped them, so that they were the victors,' 37.116.

The earlier prophets saw similar situations of exhaustion and sorrow, until they exclaimed:

> '"When comes God's help?" Ah, but surely God's help is nigh,' 2.214 (210).

Certainly this help is given, but on condition that they make their own effort:

> 'O believers, if you help God, He will help you,' 47.7 (8).

Finally God's side is victorious:

> 'Our host – they are the victors,' 37.173.

'Whoso makes God his friend, and His Messenger, and the believers – the party of God, they are the victors,' 5.56 (61).

'. . . desiring to extinguish with their mouths God's light (the reference is to those who possess scriptures); and God refuses but to perfect His light, though the unbelievers be averse.

It is He who has sent His Messenger with the guidance and the religion of truth, that he may uplift it above every religion, though the unbelievers be averse,' 9.32,33; cf. 61.8, 9; 48.28.

In short, Noah is saved from the flood, Abraham from the fire. Moses is saved from the hands of Pharaoh and his armies and Jesus from the hands of the Jews. In this way – and that is also the point of the reference to the stories of the different prophets – Muhammad will be saved and his message will triumph. Time and again the insight is that God is the one to whom this success and victory are owed. That is true both of the other prophets and of Muhammad himself. The victory which was won at Badr is due to God, 3.123 (119). They did not kill their opponents, God killed them, 8.17.

On the day of Hunayn (between Mecca and Ta'if, a battle with nomads shortly after the conquest of Mecca) it is God who sees to the victory, 9.25.

'If God helps you, none can overcome you; but if He forsakes you, who then can help you after Him? Therefore in God let the believers put all their trust,' 3.160 (154).

Punishment legends

In the second and third Meccan periods Muhammad met with growing opposition from his unbelieving Meccan fellow townsmen. It is above all in these periods that Muhammad mentions the stories of the former prophets from the Bible and from Arabia. Then he tells of Noah and the flood; Abraham's fight with polytheism; Lot and the downfall of Sodom and Gomorrah; Moses' confrontation with the Pharaoh; Hud who is sent to 'Ad; Salih to Thamud and Sju'ayb to Midian. These stories are said to be the seven events to which allusion is made in 15.87 and which are also called the punishment legends. It is a typical feature of these legends that because of unbelief and wickedness natural disasters befall each of these peoples. The following summary is given of these disasters:

'Each We seized for his sin; and of them
(a) against some We loosed a squall of pebbles
(b) and some were seized by the Cry,

(c) and some We made the earth to swallow,
(d) and some We drowned;
God would never wrong them, but they wronged themselves,' 29.40 (39).

In connection with Thamud there is also mention of an earthquake, 7.78 (76), 91 (89); 11.67 (70); in the case of Sodom and Gomorrah hail and rain bring about the downfall, 7.84 (82); 11.82 (84):

(a) The people of Lot are said to be hit by the storm wind, 54.34; a raging wind is spoken of in connection with the people of 'Ad, 41.16 (15); 54.19.
(b) Thunder (or screaming) affects the people of Thamud, 11.67 (70); the people of Midian, 11.94 (97); the people of Lot, 15.73; the people of Hijr, 15.83; the people of Noah; 23.41 (43); and unbelieving cities, 36.29 (28).
(c) The people of Korah disappeared into the earth, 28.81 (cf. Numbers 16.32).
(d) The people of Noah were drowned, 7.64 (62); 10.73 (74); 26.120; 37.82; 21.77; 25.37 (39); 11.37 (39), 43 (45); 23.27 (28); 71.25; 19.14 (13); also Pharaoh and his men, 2.50 (47); 7.136 (132); 8.54 (56); 17.103 (105); 26.66; 43.55; 44.24 (23).

Such punishments are warned of at various times. Can God also make them (others) sink into the earth, 16.45 (47), 34.9 or be drowned, 36.43? Then it is asked whether Muhammad's Meccan opponents feel safe against such a storm wind, 67.17; 17.68 (7); cf. 50.42 (41); 36.49. 53; or against such sinking, storm or drowning, 17.68, 69 (70, 71). The Meccans are warned that they can be struck by lightning, like 'Ad and Thamud, 41.13 (12).

Scheme
Some of the stories of the prophets are constructed to a particular pattern or scheme. They are as it were filtered through the experience of Muhammad himself, the career which he has so far followed as a prophet. This experience is so to speak to be read back into these stories of former prophets. Their career takes almost an identical course to that of Muhammad himself. In one way or another we see the repetition of the same drama.

Each people is sent a messenger or someone to warn them, 13.7 (8). Here both the biblical prophets and the Arabian prophets Hud, Salih and Sju'ayb appear, sent respectively to the people of 'Ad in Southern Arabia, the people of Thamud in the wadi al-Qura' and Midian. The thought is that like Muhammad himself, Hud, Salih, Sju'ayb and also Noah, Abraham and Moses had to suffer the same sarcasm and insults and threats uttered by their fellow-countrymen. The fellow-countrymen of these prophets declare their prophet a liar, mock him and refuse to accept his message. The majority of the people are punished for this, while the messenger himself is saved. This salvation comes about in the same way with Noah, 7.64 (62); Lot, 21.74; Moses, 2.50 (47); and the Arabian prophets Hud, 11.58 (61); Salih, 11.66 (69); and Sju'ayb, 11.94 (97). One by one they are saved, unlike the majority of their people.

Thus for example Muhammad, 17.47 (59), 25.8 (9) and the other prophets are regarded as 'bewitched'. Before him Moses is regarded as bewitched or as a magician, 40.24 (25); 43.49 (48). The same thing is said of Salih, 26.153 and Sju'ayb, 26.185. Muhammad too is accused of being 'possessed', 15.8; 37.36 (35); 44.14 (13); 68.51, like the others, although the Qur'an repeatedly denies that this is the case, 34.46 (45), 52.29; 68.2.; 81.22. Noah too is said to be possessed, 23.25, and likewise Moses, 26.27 (26), 51.39. Just as Muhammad is declared to be a liar, so the former communities regarded their prophets as liars, 29.18 (17). They tried to bring down messengers, like Noah, 40.5.

The stories of other prophets and the description of their experiences in the preaching of Muhammad indirectly shed light on the experiences of Muhammad himself.

Thus Sju'ayb is presented as someone who warns his people against fraudulent trading practices – precisely Muhammad's problem in Mecca, 11.84–95 (85–90); 7.85–93 (83–91).

It is said of Noah that he rejects the demands of the powerful in his community who want him to detach himself from the socially weak. If he does this, the economically strong will certainly join him. In this connection a situation is described which corresponds to that with which Muhammad saw himself confronted.

Even the old Arabian gods are presented as gods of the contemporaries of Noah, 71.23.

Abraham

The figure of Abraham occupies an extremely important place in the Qur'an. When Muhammad discusses with the people of the book, Jews and Christians, he refers to Abraham.

Abraham and his father

The Qur'an tells the story of Abraham and his father on various occasions. Like his people, Abraham's father serves idols. Abraham leaves this service for the sake of God and also tries to dissuade his father from it:

> 'And mention in the Book Abraham; surely he was a true man, a Prophet.

When he said to his father, "Father, why worshippest thou that which neither hears nor sees, nor avails thee anything?

Father, there has come to me knowledge such as came not to thee; so follow me, and I will guide thee on a level path.

Father, serve not Satan; surely Satan is a rebel against the All-merciful.

Father, I fear that some chastisement from the All-merciful will smite thee, so that thou becomest a friend to Satan."

Said he (this will mean Abraham's father), "What, art thou shrinking from my gods, Abraham? Surely, if thou givest not over, I shall stone thee; so forsake me now for some while."

He (Abraham) said, "Peace be upon thee! I will ask my Lord to forgive thee; surely He is ever gracious to me. Now I will go apart from you and that you call upon, apart from God; I will call upon my Lord, and haply I shall not be, in calling upon my Lord, unprosperous."

So, when he went apart from them and that they were serving, apart from God, We gave him Isaac and Jacob, and each We made a Prophet; and We gave them of Our mercy, and We appointed unto them a tongue of truthfulness, sublime,' 19.41–50 (42–51); cf. 2.51–67 (52–67); 26.69–77; 29.16, 17 (15,16); 37.83–98 (81–96); 43.26–28.

Abraham asks his father, who in the Qur'an is called Azar (a confusion with the name Eliezer, that of Abraham's most trusted servant, cf. Genesis 15.2; 24.2ff.?), why he takes idols as gods. He thinks that his father, like his people, is clearly in error, 6.74; cf. 21.52–54 (53–55):

'So We were showing Abraham the rule (of God) over the heavens and earth, that he might be of those having sure faith. When night outspread over him he saw a star and said, "This is my Lord." But when it set he said, "I love not the setters." When he saw the moon rising, he said, "This is my Lord." But when it set he said, "If my Lord does not guide me I shall surely be of the people gone astray." When he saw the sun rising, he said, "This is my Lord; this is greater!"

But when it set he said, "O my people, surely I am quit of that you associate. I have turned my face to Him who originated the heavens and the earth, a man of pure faith; I am not of the idolaters,"' 6.75–79.

Abraham rejects the idolatry of his father and his people, 6.74–83. Abraham prays for his father:

'Certainly I shall ask pardon for thee,' 60.4, 26; 86; 9.114 (115); 19.47 (48).

But prayer is no longer any help to someone stuck in idolatry, just as Noah's son could not be saved by the prayer of his father and perished in the flood, 11.42, 43 (44, 45), 44–47 (47–49).

Abraham prays that he and his sons may be preserved from idolatry, 14.35 (38).

The people want to burn Abraham, but God saves him by making the fire cold, 21.68–70; 29.24 (23); 37.97, 98 (95, 96).

His people declared Abraham a liar. Other peoples also declared their prophet a liar. The same fate befalls Muhammad, 22.42–44 (43).

Abraham's faith

Abraham asks at a good moment, cf. 2.258 (260), for God to show him how he can bring the dead to life:

> 'And when Abraham said, "My Lord, show me how Thou wilt give life to the dead," He said, "Why, dost thou not believe?" "Yes," he (Abraham) said, 'but that my heart may be at rest." Said He (God), "Take four birds, and twist them to thee, then set a part of them on every hill, then summon them, and they will come to thee running. And do thou know that God is All-mighty, All-wise,"' 2.260 (262) (cf. Genesis 15.8ff., where, however, the story to be seems only in the far distance).

Abraham's descendants

Abraham asks God to give him descendants. He is indeed given a son, 37.100–102 (98–100).

The angels who visit Abraham as guests announce to him the birth of a son, 15.53; 51.28 who is called Isaac, 37.112. His wife laughs at the announcement of Isaac and Jacob, 11.71 (74). She does not believe in the announcement because she is an old woman and her spouse is an old man. How can something so wonderful happen, 11.71, 72; 51.29?

But Abraham gets Isaac and Jacob as descendants, 6.84; 19.49 (50); 21.72; 29.27 (26); 14.39 (41); both will be made prophets, 19.49 (50).

Remarkable though it may sound, the information about Ishmael in the Qur'an is very limited. That is all the more surprising if one thinks what a great role he began to play in Islamic tradition as the ancestor of Quraysh, the tribe which inhabited Mecca and from which Abraham himself came.

All that is said in the Qur'an about Ishmael is that he is the son of Abraham, 14.39 (41) and that he is a messenger and prophet, 19.54 (55). He is mentioned several items in the summary list of the prophets, 4.163 (161); 6.86; 21.85; 38.48. It is especially said of him in the Qur'an that he built the Ka'ba with Abraham, 21.25, 127 (119, 121) (see below). However, in the Qur'an Ishmael clearly stands in the shadow of Abraham.

Abraham's sacrifice
In chapter 37 of the Qur'an Abraham's sacrifice is mentioned, but at least in the direct description there is no mention of which son it was whom Abraham was said to have been ready to sacrifice, Only some time after the key passage is the name of Isaac given.

> 'Then We gave him the good tidings of Isaac, a Prophet, one of the righteous,' 37.112.

It could be concluded from this that the same son is meant in the preceding passage. But the opposite can also be argued, that the son not mentioned earlier will be Ishmael and the other son mentioned later Isaac. Be this as it may, popular Islamic tradition, though not always, has thought of Ishmael as the son whom Abraham was ready to sacrifice:

> 'He (Abraham) said, "I am going to my Lord; He will guide me.
> My Lord, give me one of the righteous."
> Then We gave him the good tidings of a prudent boy.
> And when he had reached the age of running with him,
> he said, "My son, *I see in a dream* that I shall sacrifice thee; consider, what thinkest thou?" He said, "My father, do as thou art bidden; thou shalt find me, God willing, one of the steadfast."
> When they had surrendered, and he flung him upon his brow. . .
> (and then the Qur'an so to speak holds its breath)
> We called unto him, "Abraham, thou hast confirmed the vision; even so We recompense the good-doers. This is indeed the manifest trial." And We ransomed him with a mighty sacrifice,' 37.99–107 (97–107).

It is striking that the son agrees with the proposed sacrifice. In this part, obedience to the will of God is central.

According to the story in the Qur'an, Abraham is given orders in a dream to sacrifice his son.

Abraham and Lot
Abraham is told of the punishment that the people of Lot are to expect and how the inhabitants of the cities (Sodom and Gomorrah) will be swallowed up, 29.30, 31. Abraham pleads for them, but he is told that God has already made His decision, 11.74–76 (77,78); 15.57,58 (Genesis 18.31–33). However, Lot and his relatives, with the exception of Lot's wife, 15.59, 60; 29.32,33 (31,32). are saved by God because his is the only household of the submissive (i.e. Muslims), 51.36.

Abraham and the building of the Ka'ba with Ishmael

Only in the Qur'an does the story of how Abraham built the house of God in Mecca, the Ka'ba, with his son Ishmael, appear:

> 'And when We appointed the House to be a place of visitation for the people, and a sanctuary, and: "Take to yourselves Abraham's station for a place of prayer." And We made covenant with Abraham and Ishmael: "Purify My House for those that shall go about it and those that cleave to it, to those who bow and prostrate themselves,"' 2.125 (119).

> 'And when Abraham, and Ishmael with him, raised up the foundations of the House: "Our Lord, receive this from us; Thou art the All-hearing, the All-knowing,"' 2.127 (121); cf. 22.26 (27).

After the building of the Ka'ba Abraham prayed the following prayer:

> 'And when Abraham said, "My Lord, make this place (namely Mecca with the Ka'ba) secure, and turn me and my sons away from serving idols . . .
>
> Our Lord, I have made some of my seed to dwell in a valley where is no sown land by Thy Holy House; Our Lord, let them perform the prayer, and make hearts of men yearn towards them, and provide them with fruits; haply they will be thankful.
>
> Our Lord, Thou knowest what we keep secret and what we publish; from God nothing whatever is hidden in earth and heaven. Praise be to God, who has given me, though I am old, Ishmael and Isaac; surely my Lord hears the petition. My Lord, make me a performer of the prayer, and of my seed, Our Lord, and receive my petition. Our Lord, forgive Thou me and my parents, and the believers, upon the day when the reckoning shall come to pass,"' 14.35–41 (38–42).

Abraham is the one who according to the Qur'an is instructed to announce the pilgrimage in which circling the Ka'ba occupies such an important place, 22.27–29 (28–30).

Abraham's special position

After Adam, Noah and the house of Amram, God has chosen the house of Abraham above the other inhabitants of the world, 3.33 (30); cf. 19.58 (59):

> 'Yet We gave the people of Abraham the Book and the Wisdom, and We gave them a mighty kingdom,' 4.54 (57).

The prophecy and the book are entrusted to Abraham's descendants.

The 'scrolls' of Abraham and those of Moses are mentioned, 53.36, 37 (37, 38):

> 'And God took Abraham for a friend,' 4.125 (124) (cf. Isaiah 41.8; II Chronicles 20.7; James 2.23).

He is one of the elect who in later life will belong among the blessed, 2.130 (124); 16.122 (123); 29.17 (26). Like Isaac, he is blessed by God, 37.133.

Abraham submissive (muslim)
Those who follow the teachings of father Abraham are called 'submissive', i.e. Muslims in the original sense of the word. That is a name which according to the Qur'an is already used before Muhammad's time, and now again in the time of Muhammad, 22.78 (77).
The relationship of Muhammad's preaching to that of the people of the book is expressed in the following passage with a reference to Abraham:

> 'People of the Book! Why do you dispute concerning Abraham? The Torah was not sent down, neither the Gospel, but after him. What, have you no reason?
>
> Ha, you are the ones who dispute on what you know; why then dispute you touching a matter of which you know not anything? God knows, and you know not.
>
> No; Abraham in truth was not a Jew, neither a Christian; but he was a *hanif* (monotheist), a submissive one (*muslim*); certainly he was never of the idolaters,' 3.65–67 (58–60); cf. 16.120 (121), 123 (124); 2.135 (129); 3.95 (89); 6.161 (162); 6.79; 4.125.

Abraham and Muhammad

> 'Surely the people standing closest to Abraham are those who followed him, and this Prophet, and those who believe; and God is the Protector of the believers,' 3.68 (61).

In the Qur'an Abraham and those who were with him are said to be a model for believers, 60.4:

> 'You have had a good example in them for whoever hopes for God and the Last Day,' 60.6.

Jesus is presented as a model for the children of Israel, 43.59 (although here another Arab word is used for model).

It is said of Muhammad himself in almost synonymous terms:

> 'You have had a good example in God's Messenger for whosoever hopes for God and the Last Day, and remembers God oft,' 33.21.

After mentioning Abraham, Isaac, Jacob, Noah, David, Solomon, Job, Joseph, Moses, Aaron, Zechariah, John (the Baptist), Jesus, Elijah, Ishmael, Jonah and Lot, the relevant passage ends:

> 'Those are they whom God has guided; so follow their guidance,' 6.90.

Muhammad is mentioned alongside Noah, Abraham, Moses and Jesus as someone who has made a covenant with God. Only of Abraham is it said that he was a friend of God, 4.125 (124). It remains specific to Muhammad, and is not said of any other prophet in the Qur'an, that he is the seal of the prophets, 3.40, and also:

> 'We have not sent thee, save as a mercy unto all beings,' 21.107.

Passages to look up

It is interesting and instructive to investigate how the 'scheme' of Muhammad's own prophetic activity given above is reflected in that of other prophets. The stories about the Arab prophet Sju'ayb could be read in this connection, 7.85–92 (83–91); 11.84–94 (85–97). Above all the comparison between Muhammad's appearance and that of Noah is noted in this connection, 7.59–64 (57–62); 11.25–35 (27–37).

To see how Muhammad's difficult relationship with the leading circles of his Quraysh tribe is reflected in other prophets, we must note how the 'notables' (*mala)* are spoken of. Thus these stories indirectly give information about Muhammad's own experience with the unbelieving Meccans. See the 'notables' of the people of Noah, 11.27 (29), 38 (40); 23.24,33 (34); 7.60 (58); the people of 'Ad, 7.66 (74); the people of Midian, 7.88 (86), 90 (88); the people of Thamud, 7.75 (73); the people of Pharaoh, 7.109 (106), 127 (124); 26.34 (35); 28.20 (19).

Chapter 12 of the Qur'an is wholly devoted to the story of Joseph. Joseph appears outside it only a few times in the Qur'an, 6.84 and 40.33–36. It is a narrative with a strong tinge of fable. The events in the life of Joseph are bound up with the will of God more strongly than in the Bible. The Qur'an tells how God preserves his prophet in a miraculous way. The story is meant to give an example to those who have insight, 12.111. (Relations between Joseph and Potiphar's wife Suleika, though this name is not given in the Qur'an, have developed into a whole legend in the Islamic tradition. That the love is not consummated is seen as a special blessing from God.)

If you are familiar with the stories of Joseph from Genesis 37.39–50 it is instructive to read this chapter of the Qur'an and note where it agrees with the biblical narrative and where it differs from it. This brings out the specific character of this narrative in the Qur'an even better.

8

Belief and Unbelief

'O Messenger, let them not grieve thee that vie with one another in unbelief, such men as say with their mouths "We believe" but their hearts believe not,' 5.41 (45).

'Therefore in God let the believers put all their trust,' 3.160 (154).

'Say: "O unbelievers,
I serve not what you serve
and you are not serving what I serve,
nor am I serving what you have served;
neither are you serving what I serve.
To you your religion, and to me my religion!"', 109.1–6.

Introduction
In the Qur'an people are called on to submit to God. Islam is the word for that. Whoever is submissive to God is a *muslim*. Abraham is an example of this. But the Qur'an also calls for faith. It can be that a *muslim* proves to be Muslim outwardly, without really being a believer. Patience is one of the aspects of this faith. However, faith must also emerge from the deeds that one does. If one has done wrong, the way is open to repentance and turning to God. To understand precisely what the Qur'an understands by belief it is good to note the meaning of the opposite, unbelief. Ingratitude is a basic characteristic of unbelief. As well as believers and unbelievers, the Qur'an also mentions the hypocrites which stand between, but often prove to be no better than unbelievers.

Abraham as muslim
The expression that is used to denote the religion of Muslims is *islam*. Literally it means 'submission', 'submission to God':

'The true religion with God is Islam,' 3.19 (17); cf. 5.3 (5).

In this connection it is interesting to listen to the description of Abraham in the Qur'an:

'And when Abraham, and Ishmael with him, raised up the foundations of the House (what is meant is the Ka'ba in Mecca which according to the Muslim tradition was originally built by both of them), he (Abraham) said: "Our Lord, receive this from us; Thou art the All-hearing, the All-knowing; and, our Lord, make us submissive to Thee, and of our seed a nation submissive to Thee,' 2.27 28 (121,122).

The word that is twice used here is derived from the root 'submit' (*slm*, from which both Islam and Muslim are also derived). Later we hear:

'When his Lord said to him, "Submit," he said, "I have submitted me to the Lord of all Being." And Abraham charged his sons with this and Jacob likewise: "My sons, God has chosen for you the religion; see that you die not save in submission,"' 2.131, 132 (125, 126).

This 'submission' is the true religion, namely truly trusting in God.

Abraham is a prime example of this:

'Surely, Abraham was nation (in himself) obedient unto God, a man of pure faith (a monotheist, *hanif*) and no idolater, 16.120.

In the case of Abraham this is not Islam in the present sense of the word, as a designation for the Muslim religion or community. It simply indicates that at its deepest, religion is and must be about 'submission' to God. So Abraham is called a Muslim and in this sense he is exemplary. Other prophets can be called 'Muslims', and it can be said that the heart of their message is 'Islam':

'Say: "We believe in God, and that which has been sent down on us, and sent down on Abraham and Ishmael, Isaac and Jacob, and the Tribes (of Israel), and in that which was given to Moses and Jesus, and the Prophets, of their Lord; we make no division between any of them, and to Him we are submissive (*muslim*). Whoso desires another religion than Islam, it shall not be accepted of him; in the next world he shall be among the losers,' 3.84.85 (78,79).

Someone who submits and in this sense is a *muslim* is someone who gives up all selfishness and pride in human power. He is humble and gentle. He is a servant of God, an *'Abd Allah*, who submits to God as his lord and master and who knows that he is dependent on God.

The un-Muslim attitude is that of someone who is self-sufficient and who thinks that he is so rich that he has no need for help, even from God. This is the attitude of someone who thinks himself rich and trusts only in his own capacities.

'No. Man is truly arrogant, because he thinks himself sufficient,' 96.6,7; cf. 80.5

Such an attitude of self-sufficiency is the opposite of what being a Muslim means and the opposite of what it really means to fear God:

> 'As for him who gives and is godfearing and confirms the reward most fair, We shall surely ease him to the Easing. But as for him who is a miser, and self-sufficient, and cries lies to the reward most fair, We shall surely ease him to the Hardship; his wealth shall not avail him when he perishes,' 92.5–11.

Muslim and believer (mu'min)

The Qur'an makes it clear that not everyone who *says* that he submits is a automatically a 'muslim', a real believer. The Qur'an says that not every muslim is a believer (*mu'min*).

> 'The Arabs (this means the Bedouins) say, "We believe." Say: "You do not believe; rather say, 'We submit'; for belief has not yet entered your hearts,"' 49.14; cf. 9.97 (98); 5.41 (45); 48.11.

What are the characteristics of a believer? What is a true believer? The Qur'an itself gives an answer to this:

> 'The believers are those who believe in God and His Messenger, then have not doubted, and have struggled (the word *jihad* is used here) with their possessions and their selves in the way of God; those – they are the truthful ones (or the upright),' 49.15.

> 'Those only are believers who, when God is mentioned, their hearts quake, and when His signs are recited to them, it increases them in faith, and in their Lord they put their trust, those who perform the prayer (*salat*), and expend of what We have provided them, those in truth are the believers,' 8.3,4.

The Qur'an respects true believers:

> 'Those who repent, those who serve (God), those who pray, those who journey, those who bow, those who prostrate themselves (to God: the different phases or movements of ritual prayer, *salat*), those who bid to honour and forbid dishonour, those who keep God's bounds – and give thou good tidings to the believers,' 9.112 (113).

In the Qur'an, belief is often described as trust.

> '. . . and in God let the believers put all their trust. And why should we not put our trust in God, seeing that He has guided us (messengers) in our ways? We will surely endure patiently, whatever you

hurt us; and in God let all put their trust who put their trust,' 14.11, 12 (14, 15); cf. 5.23 (26).

It is also said of Joseph that he trusted God, and others are called on to do so:

'In Him I have put my trust; and in Him let all put their trust who put their trust,' 12.67.

Patience

Patience is an essential aspect of faith in God. Patience is brought to the fore above all in unfavourable circumstances and in times of testing. Much patience was required of the first followers of Muhammad and of Muhammad himself, above all in the first period in Mecca.

Patience is needed above all in the case of hostility from opponents:

'So be thou patient under what they (the unbelievers) say, and proclaim thy Lord's praise before the rising of the sun, and before its setting,' 50.69 (38); cf.20.130; 73.10.

'And restrain thyself with those who call upon their Lord at morning and evening, desiring His countenance, and let not thine eyes turn away from them, desiring the adornment of the present life,' 18.28 (27).

'O all you who believe, seek you help in patience and prayer (*salat*); surely God is with the patient,' 2.153 (148); cf. 2.45 (42).

'Surely We will try you with something of fear and hunger, and diminution of goods and lives and fruits; yet give thou good tidings unto the patient who, when they are visited by an affliction, say, "Surely we belong to God, and to Him we return,"' 2.155, 156 (151, 152).

Faith and works

Having faith and doing works of righteousness and love in human relationships are closely connected in the Qur'an. Serving God and feeding the poor are often mentioned in the same breath. In other words, piety is shown by doing right to one's fellow human beings. Piety, doing good works and true belief belong together. Belief that is worth its name is belief that expresses itself in deeds:

'And those that believe, and do deeds of righteousness – those are the inhabitants of Paradise; there they shall dwell forever,' 2.82 (76); cf. 47.12 (13), 39; 15.16.

'You will not attain piety until you expend of what you love; and whatever thing you expend, God knows of it,' 3.92 (86).

'It is not piety, that you turn your faces (at prayer) to the East and to the West. True piety is this: to believe in God, and the Last Day, the angels, the Book, and the Prophets, to give of one's substance, however cherished, to kinsmen, and orphans, the needy, the traveller, beggars, and to ransom the slave, to perform the prayer (*salat*), to pay the alms (*zakat*). And they who fulfil their covenant when they have engaged in a covenant, and endure with fortitude misfortune, hardship and peril, these are they who are true in their faith, these are the truly godfearing,' 2.177(172).

'Or do those who commit evil deeds think that We shall make them as those who believe and do righteous deeds, equal their living and their dying? How ill they judge!,' 45.21 (20).

'And some of the Arabians (Bedouins) who dwell around you (Muhammad) are hypocrites; ... And other have confessed their sins; they have mixed a righteous deed with another evil. It may be that God will turn towards them,' 9.101, 102 (102 ,103); cf. 29.7 (6).

'Those who disbelieve and bar from God's way, God will send their works astray. But those who believe and do righteous deeds and believe in what is sent down to Muhammad – and it is the truth from their Lord – He will acquit them of their evil deeds, and dispose their minds aright,' 47.1, 2.

'And when We took compact with the children of Israel:
"You shall not serve any save God;
and to be good to parents, and the near kinsman,
and to orphans, and to the needy;
and speak good to men, and perform the prayer (*salat*),
and pay the alms (*zakat*)."
Then you turned away,' 2.83 (77).

This passage contains elements from the Ten Commandments, from both the so-called first and second tables of the law: having no other gods before his face, honouring your father and your mother, and not bearing any false witness, which here is stated in a positive way (as it is also, for example, in the exposition of the Heidelberg Catechism).

At the same time, although this passage is about the Jews, the obligations are also mentioned which will develop specifically into two of the pillars of Islam, namely *salat* and *zakat*. Spirituality (*salat*) and activity (*zakat*) are closely connected, 2.277.

Unbelief as ingratitude

To discover what the Qur'an understands by belief it is instructive to note what is understood by the opposite, namely unbelief, 27.40; 39.7 (9); 14.7.

The basic meaning of the word that is translated unbelief and unbeliever is ingratitude, ungrateful. An unbeliever is someone who is ungrateful for something that has been done or some favour that has been shown. The Qur'an says that most people are ungrateful, 12.38. Just as humility is an essential element in belief, so ingratitude is the basis of unbelief, cf. 2.45,46 (42,43); 17.107–109 (108, 109).

The point turns on ingratitude to God and the goodness and favour which are shown by Him. The signs *(ayat)* of God are so many proofs of His grace and goodness. To be *grateful* to God and to *believe* in God are virtual synonyms in the Qur'an:

> 'God has struck a similitude: a city that was secure, at rest, its provision coming to it easefully from every place, then it was *ungrateful* for the blessings of God; so God let it taste the garment of hunger and of fear, for the things that they (the inhabitants of the city) were working,' 16.112 (113).

> 'So eat of what God has provided you awful and good; and be you *grateful* for the blessing of God, if it be Him that you serve,' 16.114 (115).

> 'So remember Me, and I will remember you; and be thankful to Me; and be you not ungrateful towards Me,' 2.152 (147).

In this last verse the relevant word could also be translated 'unbeliever', but it is good also to let the basic meaning come through in the translation where possible.

The Qur'an makes it clear that human ingratitude comes to light above all when the need is past:

> 'Your Lord it is who drives for you the ships on the sea that you may seek His bounty; surely He is All-compassionate towards you. And when affliction visits you upon the sea, then there go astray those on whom you call except Him; and when He delivers you to land, you turn away; man is ever ungrateful,' 17.66, 67 (68, 69).

> 'When they embark in the ships, they call on God; making their religion sincerely his; but when He has delivered them to the land, they associate others with Him (become polytheists), that they may be ungrateful for what We have given them, and take their enjoyment; they will soon know!,' 29.65,66.

> 'And when We let man taste mercy from us, he rejoices in it; but if

some evil befalls him for that his own hands have forwarded, then surely man is ungrateful,' 42.48 (47).

People are called on to count their blessings. There is a whole series of 'signs' which God gives to human beings. Despite that, they neglect the duty to be grateful. But these signs are given precisely so that they may perhaps become grateful, 16.14; cf. 16.3–18:

> 'It is God who created the heavens and the earth, and sent down out of heaven water wherewith he brought forth fruits to be your sustenance. And He subjected to you the ships to run upon the sea at His commandment; and He subjected to you the rivers and He subjected to you the sun and moon constant upon their courses, and He subjected to you the night and day, and gave you of all you asked Him. If you count God's blessing, you will never number it; surely man is sinful, ungrateful!,' 14.32, 33, 34.

The Qur'an mentions countless other favours of God, ranging from coming forth from the womb, through being given hearing, sight and strength of mind, to being given protection against the sun. Despite that:

> 'They recognize the blessing of God, then they deny it, and the most of them are the ungrateful,' 16.83 (85); cf. 16.78–83 (80–85).

Unbelief

Sometimes the Arabic words *kufr* and *kafir* must be translated unbelief and unbeliever (and not ingratitude and ungrateful). This is above all the case when the words are used as the opposite of faith or believer:.

> 'How shall God guide a people who become unbelieving (*kafaru*) after they believed, and bore witness that the messenger is true, and the clear sign came to them?,' 3.86 (80).

> 'Surely those who disbelieve after they have believed and then increase in unbelief – their repentance shall not be accepted,' 3.90 (84).

> '. . . And if thou dost follow their caprices, after the knowledge that has come to thee, thou shalt have no protector against God, and no defender,' 13.37; cf. 30.19 (28); 2.109 (103); 34.31 (30); 2.89–91 (83–85).

The Qur'an describes the spiritual state of the unbeliever in different ways. The hearts of those who believe are calm and peaceful in recalling God:

'Those who believe, their hearts being at rest in God's remembrance – in God's remembrance are at rest the hearts of those who believe,' 13.28.

But the heart of the unbeliever is described as being as hard as stone:

'Then your hearts became hardened thereafter and are like stones,' 2.74 (69).

The Qur'an says not only that the heart of the unbeliever is hardened but also that there is a veil or division between the heart and revelation, 41.3–5 (2–4); 17.45, 46 (47, 48).

In this connection there is also mention of sealing the heart of the unbeliever, cf. 2.6,7 (5,6); 9.93 (94), of veils which rest on his heart, 47.24 (26), or of rust that has got into his heart, 83.14. The unbelievers are also said to be blind and deaf, 46.26 (25):

'What, have they not journeyed in the land so that they have hearts to understand with or ears to hear with? It is not the eyes that are blind, but blind are the hearts within the breasts,' 22.46 (45); cf. 8.20–23; 2.171 (166); 6.25; 2.171 (166):

Instead of remembering, God's people are forgetful. The Qur'an wants to remind them of what they constantly risk forgetting. With a word-play in Arabic, man (*insan*) is described as forgetful (*nisyan).* Forgetfulness is clearly a fundamental human characteristic:

'Be not as those who forgot God, and so He caused them to forget their souls; those – they are the ungodly,' 59.19; cf. 32.14; 45.34 (33); 7.51 (49); 9.67 (68).

Hypocrisy

In addition to believers and unbelievers, the Qur'an also speaks of a third category of people, namely the hypocrites. This roughly means that they (the hypocrites) confess belief outwardly but have remained unbelievers in their hearts:

'The hypocrites, the men and the women, are as one another; they bid to dishonour, and forbid honour; they keep their hands shut; they have forgotten God, and He has forgotten them. The hypocrites – they are the ungodly,' 9.67 (68).

'O Prophet, struggle with the unbelievers and the hypocrites, and be thou harsh with them; their refuge shall be Gehenna – an evil homecoming!,' 66.9.

So the hypocrites stand somewhere between the extreme poles of belief and unbelief, though they are then sometimes, 66.9, mentioned in the same breath as the unbelievers:

> 'The hypocrites seek to trick God, but God is tricking them. When they stand up to pray (*salat*) they stand up lazily, showing off to the people and not remembering God save a little,' 4.142 (141); cf. 2.264 (266) and Matthew 6.5.

> 'Upon the day when the hypocrites, men and women, shall say to those who have believed, "Wait for us, so that we may borrow your light!", it shall be said, "Return you back behind, and seek for a light!" . . . They (the hypocrites) shall be calling unto them (the believers), "Were we not with you?" They shall say, "Yes indeed; but you tempted yourselves, and you awaited, and you were in doubt, and fancies deluded you, until God's commandment came, and the Deluder deluded you concerning God,"' 57.13,14 (13).

(This last story suggests the parable of the wise and foolish virgins. The foolish virgins also had no more light and asked the wise for some, Matthew 25.1–13.)

The word hypocrite originally seems to have been used for some citizens of Medina who joined Muhammad after he emigrated from Mecca to Medina. In sharp contrast to those who follow God's emissary with an unshakeable belief in God, these people of Medina are cunning, hesitant and real opportunists. This term is first applied to people of that type. Chapter 9 of the Qur'an describes some Arabians like this:

> 'The Arabians (the Bedouins) are more stubborn in unbelief and hypocrisy, and appear not to know the bounds of what God has sent down on His Messenger,' 9.97 (98); cf. 2.101 (102).

It is the people who have a sickness in their heart, 2.10 (9): although they pretend to be believers, they are hypocrites. The hypocrite is the one who outwardly is perhaps a pious Muslim, but in his heart he remains an unbeliever and is clearly hostile to God and His Prophet.

The opposite of a hypocrite is someone who is trustworthy (*sadiq*), 33.23, 24.

Passages to look up

It is impossible always to determine the circumstances in which particular verses have been revealed. Far less are the 'causes of the revelation', as they are called, always known. However, it is clear that the expressions about belief, unbelief and hypocrisy are also used in the

Qur'an in connection with attitudes and specific people in Muhammad's surroundings.

For the attitude of the Bedouins in the last years of Muhammad's activity, cf. 9.97–106 (98–107).

For the attitude of hypocrisy, cf. 3.167 (161), in connection with the battle of Uhud.

The theme of gratitude occurs often in the Qur'an, as does its opposite. For yet more pictures compare 80.16-(23); 22.66 (65); 29.67; 67.23; 39.66; 7.10 (9); 23.78 (80); 32.9 (8); 76.3.

9

Man in the Qur'an: The Story of Adam

'O mankind, We have created you male and female, and appointed you races and tribes, that you may know one another. Surely the noblest among you in the sight of God is the most godfearing of you. God is All-knowing, All-aware,' 49.13.

'We created man in affliction,' 90.4.

Introduction

The Qur'an is addressed to human beings. God is the 'Lord of men', 'king of men' and 'God of men', as the closing chapter of the Qur'an explains, 114.1–3.

The Qur'an is very much under the impact of the creation of human beings and sees here a proof that the God who can create can also re-create, i.e. at the resurrection of the dead. The creation of human beings and the world is not without a plan or goal. Human beings are servants of God. The Qur'an does not pass over the greatness and misery of human beings. Human beings have responsibility. Gratitude must be their basic attitude.

Adam was created as the first man, the representative, *kalif*, of God on earth. But man sinned, and is confronted with Satan as his permanent enemy. The story of Adam is meant to be a lesson for all his children.

The creation of man

In the Qur'an it is said of man that the Compassionate One has created him, 55.3 (2). It is certainly said that man is created in affliction, 90.4. Unlike other creatures, God has breathed man's spirit into him and provided him with hearing, sight and mental capacity, 32.9 (78); cf. 16.78 (80); 23; 78 (80); 67.23. Man is created, when at first he did not exist, 19.9 (10), 67 (68).

Man is created of one soul and from man his spouse, 4.1; 6.98; 7.189; 39.6.

It is God who has created the two spouses, male and female, from one drop of ejaculated seed, 53.45; 46 (46,47); cf. 31.11 (12); 75.39; 78.8.

Human beings are created of mud, 6.2; 7.12 (11), 23.12; 32.7 (6); 37.11; 38.71; or of clay, 15.26, 28; 55.14 (13); of matter, 3.59 (52); 18.37 (35); 22.5; 35.11 (12); 40.67 (69).

Man is created from a drop of sperm, 18.37 (35), 22,5; 23.13; 35.11,12; 36; 77; 40.67 (69); 75.37; 76.2; 80.19 (18); from moisture, 32.8 (7); 77.20; 86.6; from an embryo, 22.5; 23.14; 40.67–79; 96.2.

On various occasions the Qur'an describes the whole biological process:

> 'It is He who created you of dust then of a sperm-drop, then of a blood-clot, then He delivers you as infants, then that you may come of age, then that you may be old men – though some of you there are who die before it – and that you may reach a stated term; haply you will understand,' 40.67 (69).

> 'We created man of an extraction of clay, then We set him, a drop, in a receptacle secure, then We created of the drop (sperm) a clot, then We created of the clot a tissue, then We created of the tissue bones, then We garmented the bones in flesh; thereafter We produced him as another creature. So blessed be God, the fairest of creators!,' 23.12–14; cf. 32.7–9 (6–8); 35.11 (12); 39.6 (8); 35.11 (12).

For people who doubt the possibility of the resurrection of the dead, reference is made to this biological process as a proof and a sign of the resurrection:

> 'O men, if you are in doubt as to the Uprising, surely We created you of dust then of a sperm-drop, then of a blood-clot, then of a lump of flesh, formed and unformed that We may make clear to you. And We establish in the wombs what We will, till a stated term, then We deliver you as infants, then that you may come of age; and some of you die, and some of you are kept back unto the vilest state of life, that after knowing somewhat, they may know nothing. And thou beholdest the earth blackened, then, when We send down water upon it, it quivers, and swells, and puts forth herbs of every joyous kind. That is because God – He is the truth, and brings the dead to life, and is powerful over everything,' 22.5, 6.

No aimless creation

According to the Qur'an the creation of man was not more difficult for God than that of heaven, 79.27. Just as the creation of the heavens and earth are part of God's signs, 49.29 (28), so the creation of man is a sign for those who are sure in their faith, 45.4 (3); cf. also 2.164 (159); 31.30. Just as it is also said of heaven and earth that they were not created as a game, 21.16; 44.38; or vainly, 38.27, but in truth (for a real purpose), 15.85; 46.3.2; 30.8 (7); 6.73(72), so it was no whim to create human beings:

> 'What, did you think that We created you only for sport (without a purpose), and that you would not be returned to Us?', 23.115 (117).

God does not leave man unnoticed, 75.36; 76.1. God leads him on the way, grateful or ungrateful. According to the Qur'an man is religious by 'nature':

> 'So set thy face to the religion, a man of pure faith (*hanif*, or monotheist) – God's original upon which He originated mankind. There is no changing God's creation. That is the right religion; but most men know it not,' 30.30 (29).

Man God's servant

The Qur'an says that man is created to serve God, 51.56. He is a servant of God, '*Abd Allah*. There is no being in heaven or on earth who does not come to the Compassionate One as servant, 19.93 (4); cf. 21.26. The angels are also called servants of God, 21.26. Already in the cradle Jesus is declared to be a servant of God, 19.30 (31):

> 'He is only a servant We blessed, and We made him to be an example,' 43.59.

> 'The Messiah will not disdain to be a servant of God, neither the angels who are near stationed to Him,' 4.172 (170) (cf. Philippians 2.7).

Muhammad is also called a servant, 17.1; cf. 57.9; 72.19. The Qur'an describes the servants of God as follows:

> 'The servants of the All-merciful are those who walk in the earth modestly and who, when the ignorant address them, say, "Peace"; who pass the night prostrate to their Lord and standing; who say, "Our Lord, turn Thou from us the chastisement of Gehenna; surely its chastisement is torment most terrible; evil it is as a lodging-place and an abode"; who, when they expend, are neither prodigal nor parsimonious, but between that is a just stand.
>
> Who call not upon another god with God, nor slay the soul God has forbidden except by right, neither fornicate, for whosoever does that shall meet the price of sin – doubled shall be the chastisement for him on the Resurrection Day, and he shall dwell therein humbled, save him who repents, and believes, and does righteous work – those, God will change their evil deeds into good deeds, for God is ever All-forgiving, All-compassionate.
>
> And whosoever repents, and does righteousness, he truly turns to God in repentance.
>
> And those who bear not false witness and, when they pass by idle talk, pass by with dignity;

Who, when they are reminded of the signs of their Lord, fall not down thereat deaf and blind; who say, "Our Lord, give us refreshment of our wives and seed, and make us a model to the god-fearing."

Those shall be recompensed with the highest heaven, for that they endured patiently, and they shall receive therein a greeting and – Peace (*salam*)!

Therein they shall dwell forever; fair it is as a lodging-place and an abode,' 25.63–76 (64–76).

It is said of God that the looks sharply at his servants, 3.15 (13), 20 (19); 40.44 (47). He is kind to them, 2.207 (203); 3.30 (28). It is said of Satan that he cannot mislead the servants of God, 15.39, 40; 38.82, 83 (83, 84). God will pass judgment on his servants, 40.48 (51) but, as it is said, he does not intend to do injustice to his servants, 40.31 (33); cf.3.182 (187); 8.51 (53); 41.46; 50.29.

'Greatness and misery'

Man occupies a special place in the Qur'an. At the end of His work of creation God says:

'We offered the trust to the heavens and the earth and the mountains, but they refused to carry it and were afraid of it; and man carried it. Surely he is sinful, very foolish,' 33.72.

Man proves to be someone who does not do what God has commanded him, 80.23. Man wreaks corruption on land and sea, 30.41 (40). He openly seeks quarrels, 16.4; 36.77.

God has taken a risk in creating man:

'they have hearts, but understand not with them; they have eyes, but perceive not with them; they have ears, but they hear not with them. They are like cattle; nay, rather they are further astray. Those – they are the heedless,' 7.179 (178).

Men are even called brothers of Satan, 17.27 (29). Man is fickle, 70.19, and arrogant, and he thinks himself so rich that he has no need of help (from God), 96.6, 7.

Human responsibility

According to the Qur'an, during a man's life there are two angels who accompany him, one on his right hand and one on his left, and note what he says, and for this he will be called to account at the last judgment, 50.17, 18 21 (16, 17, 20):

'As for man, whenever his Lord tries him, and honours him, and blesses him, then he says, "My Lord has honoured me." But when he tries him and stints for him his provision, then he says, "My Lord has despised me." No indeed; but you honour not the orphan, and you urge not the feeding of the needy, and you devour the inheritance greedily, and you love wealth with an ardent love,' 89.15–20 (14–21); cf. 100.8; 102.1; 104.2,3.

Nothing will happen to a man but what he himself has done. He will be rewarded accordingly, 53.39–41 (40–42). God recompenses every soul for what he has done, 14.51; 39.70. No soul shall be treated unjustly, 36.54; cf. 20.17. No one shall bear the burden of another, 6.164; 35.18 (19); 39.7 (9); 53.58 (39). God does not burden a soul above its capacity, 2.233, 286; 6.152 (153); 7.42 (40); 23.62 (64). On earth no one would survive if God exacted retribution for their injustice and gave them what they deserved, 16.61 (63); 35.45 (44). One day hell will be full of *jinns* and men, warns the Qur'an, 11.119 (120); 32.13; 7.179 (178).

Prayer of a forty-year-old

When a man reaches the age of forty he should be grateful:

> 'We have charged man, that he be kind to his parents; his mother bore him painfully, and painfully she gave birth to him; his bearing and his weaning are thirty months. Until, when he is fully grown, and reaches forty years, he says, "O my Lord, dispose me that I may be thankful for Thy blessing wherewith Thou hast blessed me and my father and mother, and that I may do righteousness well-pleasing to Thee; and make me righteous also in my seed. Behold, I repent to Thee, and am among those that surrender,"' 46.15; cf. 31.14 (13).

The creation of Adam

Not only does the Qur'an speak of man and the creation of man; it also makes more specific statements about Adam.

The creation of Adam is compared in the Qur'an with that of Jesus. Adam created him from matter, after which he said, 'Become, and he became' 3.59 (52).

The Qur'an tells the story of Adam's creation as follows, but without mentioning him by name:

> 'And when thy Lord said to the angels, "See, I am creating a mortal of a clay of mud moulded. When I have shaped him, and breathed My spirit in him, fall you down, bowing before him!" Then the angels bowed themselves all together, save Iblis; he refused to be among those bowing. Said He, "'What ails thee, Iblis, that thou art not among those bowing?" Said he, "I would never bow myself before a mortal whom Thou hast created of a clay of mud moulded."

Said He, "Then go thou forth hence; thou art accursed. Upon thee shall rest the curse, till the Day of Doom." Said he, "My Lord, respite me till the day they shall be raised." Said He, "Thou art among the ones that are respited unto the day of a known time." Said he, "My Lord, for Thy perverting me I shall deck all fair to them in the earth, and I shall pervert them, all together, excepting those Thy servants among them that are devoted." Said He, "This is for Me a straight path: over My servants thou shalt have no authority, except those that follow thee, being perverse," 15.28–42; cf. 38.71ff.; 7.10ff.

In what is in a sense a parallel text it is also said about Iblis, in connection with his not being willing to prostrate himself before Adam, that he was haughty and belonged among the unbelievers, 38.74.

One of the explanations which Iblis gives God there for his refusal to prostrate himself before Adam (cf. also 20.116 (115); 2.34 (32); 7.11 (10); 17.61 (63); 18.50 (48)) is:

'I am better than he; Thou createdst me of fire, and him Thou createdst of clay,' 38.76 (77).

At yet another place in the Qur'an the conversation between God and the angels about planning to create man is given as follows:

'And when thy Lord said to the angels, "I am setting in the earth a viceroy," they said, "What, wilt Thou set therein one who will do corruption there, and shed blood, while We proclaim Thy praise and call Thee Holy?" He said, "Assuredly I know that you know not,"' 2.30 (28).

There is mention of a degree of rivalry between the angels and man. Man is asked to name things – naming things is describing their nature and being. The angels cannot do that, but Adam can. In the Bible Adam gives the names (Genesis 2.19), while in the Qur'an God communicates these to Adam:

'And He taught Adam the names, all of them; then he presented them unto the angels and said, "Now tell Me the names of these, if you speak truly." They said, "Glory be to Thee! We know not save what Thou hast taught us. Surely Thou art the All-knowing, the All-wise." He said, "Adam, tell them their names." And when he had told them their names He said, "Did I not tell you I know the unseen things of the heavens and earth? And I know what things you reveal, and what you were hiding,"' 2.31–33 (29–31).

Although the name of Eve is not mentioned in the Qur'an, it is alluded to:

'It is He who created you out (Adam, who here too is not mentioned by name) of one living soul, and made of him his spouse that he might rest in her,' 7.189; cf. 30.21 (20); 39.6 (8); 41; 35.11 (12); 6.98; 16.72 (74); 42.11 (9).

The fall of Adam and Eve

The Qur'an tells how Satan succeeds in causing man to fall:

> '[And God said]: "O Adam, inherit, thou and thy wife, the Garden, and eat of where you will, but come not nigh this tree, lest you be of the evildoers."
>
> Then Satan whispered to them, to reveal to them that which was hidden from them of their shameful parts. He said, "Your Lord has only prohibited you from this tree lest you become angels, or lest you become immortals." And he swore to them, "Truly, I am for you a sincere adviser." So he led them on by delusion; and when they tasted the tree, their shameful parts were revealed to them, so they took to stitching upon themselves leaves of the Garden.
>
> And their Lord called to them. "Did not I prohibit you from this tree, and say to you, 'Verily Satan is for you a manifest foe'?" They said, "Lord, we have wronged ourselves, and if Thou dost not forgive us, and have mercy upon us, we shall surely be among the lost." Said He, "Get you down, each of you an enemy to each. In the earth a sojourn shall be yours, and enjoyment for a time." Said He, "Therein you shall live, and therein you shall die, and from there you shall be brought forth,"' 7.19–25 (18–24).

At yet another place the Qur'an relates the same story as follows:

> 'And We made covenant with Adam before, but he forgot, and We found in him no constancy... Then We said, "Adam, surely this (Iblis) is an enemy to thee and thy wife. So let him not expel you both from the Garden, so that thou art unprosperous. It is assuredly given to thee neither to hunger therein, nor to go naked, neither to thirst therein, nor to suffer the sun."
>
> Then Satan whispered to him saying, "Adam, shall I point thee to the Tree of Eternity, and a Kingdom that decays not?" So the two of them ate of it, and their shameful parts revealed to them and they took to stitching upon themselves leaves of the Garden. And Adam disobeyed his Lord, and so he erred. Thereafter his Lord chose him, and turned again unto him, and He guided him. Said He, "Get you down, both of you together, out of it, each of you an enemy to each: but if there comes to you from Me guidance, then whosoever follows My guidance shall not go astray, neither shall he be unprosperous,"' 20.115 (114), 117–123 (115–122).

Satan the enemy of man

The Qur'an repeatedly makes it clear that Satan is man's enemy *par excellence*. That is brought out in various stories about prophets. Joseph's father tells his son that Satan is a declared enemy, 12.5. When Moses gets involved in a fight between an Egyptian and an Israelite, takes the side of the Israelite and kills the Egyptian, clearly unintentionally, he says:

> '"This is of Satan's doing; he is surely an enemy misleading, manifest." He said, "My Lord, I have wronged myself. Forgive me!" So God forgave him, for He is the All-forgiving, the All-compassionate,' 28.15, 16 (14, 15); cf. 20.40 (41) (Exodus 2.11, 12).

The warning not to be hindered by Satan because he is a declared enemy also appears in the story about Jesus, 43.62. Because Satan is an enemy, there is also a call to treat him as an enemy, 35.6:

> 'Made I (God) not covenant with you, Children of Adam, that you
> should not serve Satan – surely he is a manifest foe to you –
> and that you should serve Me? This is a straight path,' 36.60,61.

However, Satan is someone who stirs things up among the servants of God, 17.53 (55). But people are called not to tread in the footsteps of Satan, 2.168 (163); 2.208 (204); 6.142 (143); 24.21.

Although Satan or Iblis is an opponent of man and tries to lead him astray and distract him from the right way, in the end man is responsible for his deeds. According to the Qur'an man himself acts unjustly.

The lesson of the story

In the Qur'an it is clear that Adam is described as the prototype of man as such.

Clearly a lesson is meant to be drawn from the creation story for all the children of Adam: .

> 'Children of Adam! we have sent down on you a garment to cover your shameful parts, and feathers; and the garment of godfearing – that is better; that is one of God's signs; haply they will remember.
>
> Children of Adam! Let not Satan tempt you as he brought your parents out of the Garden, stripping them of their garments to show them their shameful parts. Surely he sees you, he and his tribe, from where you see them not. We have made the Satans the friends of those who do not believe,' 7.26,27 (25, 26)

> 'Children of Adam! If there should come to you Messengers from among you, relating to you My signs, then whosoever is godfearing and makes amends – no fear shall be on them, neither shall they sorrow,' 7.35 (33).

The Qur'an even expresses the thought that already before their birth the descendants of Adam had testified to the faith. For this it seems that man cannot excuse himself as though he had known nothing:

> 'And when thy Lord took from the Children of Adam, from their loins, their seed, and made them testify touching themselves, "Am I not your Lord?" They said, "Yes, we testify" – lest you should say on the Day of Resurrection, "As for us, we were heedless of this,"' 7.172 (171).

Passages to look up

The story of the creation of Adam and all that is connected with it is told three times in the Qur'an.

It is worth reading the different versions as a unity and then comparing them with one another. These are respectively 2.30–39 (28–37); 7.25 (9–24) (with verses 26–33 (25–31) which deal with the lesson that must be drawn from this story) and 20.115–123 (114–122).

10

The Qur'an as a Law Book

'And We have sent down to thee the Book with the truth, confirming the Book that was before it, and assuring it. So judge between them according to what God has sent down, and do not follow their caprices, to forsake the truth that has come to thee. To every one of you We have appointed a right way and an open road . . .

And judge between them according to what God has sent down, and do not follow their caprices, and beware of them lest they tempt thee away from any of what God has sent down to thee. But if they turn their backs, know that God desires only to smite them for some sin they have committed; surely, many men are ungodly.

Is it the judgment of pagandom then that they are seeking? Yet who is fairer in judgment than God, for a people having sure faith?' 5.48, 49, 50 (52, 54, 55).

Introduction

In the Islamic world the Qur'an is regarded as one of the most important sources of legislation, if not the most important.

What are the laws, regulations or precepts that the Qur'an has given?

It was above all in Medina that Muhammad developed into a political leader of a community (*umma*) of Muslims. All kinds of rules and regulations came into being; a community which really submits to God – which obeys God and his Prophet – has to submit to these regulations. An important part of the Qur'an is taken up with them, so they need separate attention.

First I shall mention some 'personal' Islamic virtues which in a sense can be regarded as a counterpart to the Ten Commandments.

The social situation in Mecca and the first preaching there clearly already form the basis for what will later be prescribed in Medina. The preaching of judgment in Mecca is already directed against the exploitation of people, among other things by the practice of usury. Later, increasingly clear instructions are given about what a 'submissive' community must require and forbid, regard as legitimate and illegitimate. In the social sphere there are regulations about the giving of alms (*zakat*), contributions and offerings, which like the usury demand a great deal; however, in this case there is a reward with God.

Finally, we shall pause over the regulations connected with the position of women, questions of inheritance and the prescriptions of penalties.

Islamic virtues

The 'Ten Commandments' are not mentioned as such in the Qur'an. But there are statements which are very similar and which stand after these commandments:

> 'Say, "Come, I will recite what your Lord has forbidden you: that you associate not anything with Him (viz. do not worship any other gods), and to be good to your parents, and not to slay your children because of poverty.
>
> We (God) will provide you and them; and that you approach not any indecency outward or inward, and that you slay not the soul God has forbidden, except by right. That then He has charged you with; haply you will understand.
>
> And that you approach not the property of the orphan, save in the fairer manner, until he is of age. And fill up the measure and the balance with justice. We charge not any soul save to its capacity. And when you speak, be just, even if it should be to a near kinsman. And fulfil God's covenant, that then He has charged you with; haply you will remember.
>
> And that this is My path, straight; so do you follow it, and follow not divers paths lest they scatter you from His path.
>
> That then He has charged you with; haply you will be godfearing,"'

6.151–153 (152–154); cf. 17.23 (24), 31 (33), 35 (34, 36).

In many passages the Qur'an commands the care of parents:

> 'We have charged man, that he be kind to his parents; his mother bore him painfully, and painfully she gave birth to him,' 46.15 (14).

> 'Thy Lord has decreed you shall not serve any but Him, and to be good to parents, whether one or both of them attains old age with thee; say not to them "Fie" neither chide them, but speak unto them words respectful,' 17.23, 24 (24.25); cf. 6.151 (152) 4.36, 37 (40).

The following is to be regarded as a list of Islamic virtues:

> 'Men and women who are submissive,
> believing men and believing women,
> obedient men and obedient women,
> truthful men and truthful women,

enduring men and enduring women,
humble men and humble women,
men and women who give in charity,
men who fast and women who fast,
men and women who guard their private parts,
men and women who remember God oft –
for them God has prepared forgiveness and a mighty wage,' 33.35.

Gratitude and repentance could also be added to them.

The social situation

In Muhammad's time the social and economic situation was particularly bad for a large part of the population. Clearly there were barbarous customs like burying girls alive, 81.8, 9; 16.58, 59 (60,61), presumably because of poverty. While Mecca itself was prosperous, the weak were exploited by the richer. There were all kinds of fraudulent trading practices. There was much callousness, selfishness, pride and lack of gentleness on the side of the rich. The Qur'an tells us that the Meccans were solely concerned with acquiring riches. They pursued this life. It was the only thing that they knew, 53.29,30 (30,31).

From the first moment, the call to observe justice and do right to the poor and oppressed resounds in Muhammad's preaching. The Qur'an attacks the disgraceful trading practices of his fellow-townsmen: their deception, exploitation and usury:

'. . . who has gathered riches and counted them over thinking his riches have made him immortal,' (104.2, 3).

The Qur'an says that once people have got a thirst for riches, it will never leave them alone. This pressure diverts them from any higher striving; the weak, poor and orphans then suffer:

'. . . you urge not the feeding of the needy, and you devour the inheritance greedily, and you love wealth with an ardent love,' 89.18,20 (19, 21).

The economic and social inequality which predominate in Meccan society is disapproved of and is found fault with above all in the preaching of judgment (see Chapter 5 above). The preaching of the one God is also directed towards restoring unity among people. Man cannot give away his possessions at will. This is expressed in the story of the Arab prophet Sju'ayb, who is sent to Midian: the story of a prophet which, as so often, at the same time says something about Muhammad and what people said to him:

'They said: "Sju'ayb, does thy prayer command thee that we should leave that our father served, or to do as we will with our goods?,"' 11.87 (89).

The community which commands the good and forbids the evil
The Qur'an divides people before the coming of Islam into two categories: the people of the book (namely Jews and Christians) and the people to whom no book is given (the so-called *ummiyun*). These groups are sharply opposed and hostile to each other. Initially the Arabians, too, belong to the second and last group, especially the idolaters or polytheists among them. Muhammad is now called in the Qur'an the *nabi al-ummi*, which is usually translated illiterate prophet, 7.157,158 (156 ,158). The most usual interpretation is that Muhammad could neither read nor write. But regardless of whether or not this was the case, the most probable meaning is that the term designates Muhammad the prophet who is sent to the *ummiyun,* those who still have no written scripture and thus in this sense are unlettered:

> 'It is He who has raised up from among the common people a Messenger from among them, to recite His signs to them and to purify them, and to teach them the Book and the Wisdom, though before that they were in manifest error,' 62.2.

That means that the Arabians, who were once among those without a scripture, have now received an Arabic revelation and so also become a 'people of the book'.

But this community, the youngest in the series, grows to be the best community:

> 'You are the best nation ever brought forth to men', 2.110 (106);

> 'God has made them a community of the middle,' 2.143 (137).

The Prophet must address himself from this 'community of the middle' both to the people who have no book and to those who already have a book:

> 'And say to those who have been given the Book and to the common folk: "Are you submissive?,"' 3.20 (19).

In the verse just quoted it is said of this community of the middle that it is 'bidding to honour and forbidding dishonour', 3.110 (106):

> 'Let there be one nation of you, calling to good, and bidding to honour, and forbidding dishonour; those (who do that) are the prosperers,' 3.104 (100).

The two terms, in Arabic *ma'ruf* and *munkar*, express what is 'commanded' and what is 'forbidden'. The first word means what is 'known' , 'familiar' and therefore 'socially acceptable'. The last word denotes the opposite, what is unknown and alien; cf. 5.78, 79 (82,83); 58.2.

In the Qur'an emphasis is regularly laid on prescribing and following what is right and forbidding what is wrong (in short, good and evil):

> 'And the believers, the men and the women, are friends one of the other; they bid to honour, and forbid dishonour; they perform the prayer, and pay the alms (*zakat*), and they obey God and His Messenger,' 9.71 (72).

The hypocrites are described as those who do precisely the opposite:

> 'The hypocrites, the men and the women, are as one another; they bid to dishonour, and forbid honour; they keep their hands shut (in other words, they give nothing); they have forgotten God, and He has forgotten them. The hypocrites – they are the ungodly,' 9.67 (68).

A pair of terms which also expresses what may or may not be done is 'forbidden' (*haram*) and 'allowed' (*halal*); cf. 2.84, 86 (78, 79). For example it is said about Jesus:

> 'I likewise confirm the truth of the Torah that is before me, and make lawful to you certain things that before were forbidden unto you,' 3.50 (44).

Clearly the thought is that new and better precepts replace those which were in force previously. According to the Qur'an, the Jewish food laws were originally imposed on the Jews to punish them for their greed, 6.146 (147), but now:

> 'These things only has He forbidden you: carrion, blood, the flesh of swine, what has been hallowed to other than God,' 2.173 (168).

> 'Permitted to you (Muslims) is the game of the sea and the food of it, as a provision for you and for the journeyers; but forbidden to you is the game of the land, so long as you remain in pilgrim sanctity (at the time of the *haj*,' 5.96 (97).

The Qur'an wants a just and righteous order to be created on earth. Therefore there is a warning against bringing corruption on earth:

> 'Do not corruption in the land, after it has been set right,' 7.56 (54).

[And to Midian their brother Sju'ayb] he said: "O my people, serve God! You have no god other than He; there has now come to you a clear sign from your Lord. So fill up the measure and the balance, and diminish not the goods of the people; and do not bring corruption in the land, after it has been set right,"'7.85 (83); cf. 11.116 (118); 12.73; 13.25; 16.88 (90); 26.152; 28.77; 2.205; 30.41.

It is not the case that Islamic society is automatically assured of being God's favourite. If it is to establish itself on earth, it must prescribe prayers, offer alms (*zakat*), command the good and forbid the evil, 22.41 (42). The Muslims are warned that:

'If you (the disciples) turn away, He will substitute another people instead of you, then they will not be your likes,' 47.38 (40).

The following verse can be read as a kind of summary of what is prescribed:

'It is not piety, that you turn your faces to the East and to the West. True piety is this: to believe in God, and the Last Day, the angels, the Book, and the Prophets, to give of one's substance, however cherished, to kinsmen, and orphans, the needy, the travellers, beggars, and to ransom the slave, to perform the prayer (*salat*), to pay the alms (*zakat*). And they who fulfil their covenant, and endure with fortitude misfortune, hardship and peril, these are they who are true in their faith, these are the truly godfearing,' 2.177 (172).

Prohibition of usury

One of the areas in which what is commanded or prohibited is focussed is that of usury. In the society in which Muhammad preached for the first time people were cast into poverty and kept in it because of the levying of exorbitant rents. It is not surprising that this is sharply condemned. Jews are mentioned as those who extract usury, although this is also strictly forbidden to them, 4.161 (159); 3.130 (125); cf. Exodus 22.24, Leviticus 25.35–37; Deuteronomy 23.20:

'Those who devour usury shall not rise again except as he rises (on the day of resurrection), whom Satan of the touch prostrates; that is because they say, "Trafficking is like usury." God has permitted (*halal*) trafficking, and forbidden (*haram*) usury,' 2.275 (276).

'God blots out usury, but freewill offerings He augments with interest,' 2.276 (277).

The Qur'an insists that no usury shall be levied and commands anyone who is guilty to give the money as an offering of love, in other words to forgive the charge, 2.278–280.

The Qur'an makes it quite clear that with God, usury produces no gain:

> 'And what you give in usury, that it may increase upon the people's wealth, increases not with God; but what you give in alms (*zakat*), desiring God's Face, those – they receive recompense manifold,' 30.39 (38).

Time and again, making offerings and giving alms are set against these practises of usury.

Almsgiving (zakat)

The Qur'an repeatedly makes it clear that the believer must give alms (*zakat*), contributions or gifts of love.

There is a repeated call to give alms (*zakat*), often made in the same breath as the call to prayer (*salat),* 2.43 (40), 83 (77), 110 (104), 177 (178); 4.77 (79); 5.12 (15), 55 (60); 9.5, 11, 18, 71 (72); 22.78 (77); 24.37, 56 (55); 27.3; 31.4 (3); 33.33; 58.13 (14); 73.20; 98.5 (4). It is the characteristic of the polytheists that they do not give *zakat*, 41.7 (6).

According to the Qur'an this is not the introduction of something new, although *zakat* will later develop into one of the pillars of Islam. The children of Israel already had the same obligation, 2.83 (77); 5.12 (15). Lot puts an obligation on his people to give alms, 21.73, and Ishmael also issues a call to do this, 19.55 (56). It is also imposed as an obligation on Jesus, 19.31 (32).

It is a call to an attitude which is diametrically opposed to that which is indicated with the levying of usury:

> '. . . men whom neither commerce nor trafficking diverts from the remembrance of God and to perform the prayer (*salat*), and to pay the alms (*zakat*), fearing a day when hearts and eyes shall be turned about,' 24.37.

The call to offer this *zakat* clearly also has its own importance. It is done for mercy to be shown, 24.56 (55):

> 'Those who believe and do deeds of righteousness, and perform the prayer (*salat*), and pay the alms (*zakat*) – their wage awaits them with their Lord, and no fear shall be on them, neither shall they sorrow,' 2.277.

> 'And perform the prayer (*salat*), and pay the alms (*zakat*); whatever good you shall forward to your souls' account, you shall find it with God; assuredly God sees the things you do,' 2.110 (104).

The Qur'an expresses roughly the same thought when it speaks of giving contributions. When the unbelievers are called on to do this they ask why they have to give food to those whom God himself can feed as he will, 36.47 (46). Unbelievers are mentioned who give offerings but do so with the opposite purpose, namely to divert people from the way of God, 8.36. It is said of hypocrites that they give offerings, but do so with the opposite intention, 9.54; cf. 4.142 (141).

However, it is the characteristic of the believer that he gives contributions from the sustenance which God has given him, 42.38 (36). What he can do without must be given, 2.219 (217). What he gives must be the virtuous things, 2.267 (269).

Even that is not all. The Qur'an goes rather further by calling on people to give what they are really attached to:

> 'You will not attain piety until you expend of what you love; and whatever thing you expend, God knows of it,' 3.92 (86).

On the one hand the Qur'an points out that these offerings must not be exaggerated; on the other hand there must not be excessive restraint either. Here the middle way needs to be taken, 25.67. And anyone who does not have need not give, 9.107 (108).

How are these offerings determined?

> 'They will question thee concerning what they should expend. Say: "Whatever good you expend is for parents and kinsmen, orphans, the needy, and the traveller; and whatever good you may do, God has knowledge of it,"' 2.215 (211).

Whatever someone gives as a contribution is to his advantage:

> 'And whatever good you expend is for yourselves, for then you are expending, being desirous only of God's Face; and whatever good you expend shall be repaid to you in full, and you will not be wronged,' 2.272 (274).

What is given as an offering forms as it were an insurance with God for later, 34.39 (38). A great reward is set aside for those who give, 57.7:

> 'Those who expend their wealth night and day, secretly and in public, their wage awaits them with their Lord, and no fear shall be on them, neither shall they sorrow,' 2.274 (275); cf. 13.22; 14.31 (36); 2.254 (255).

The Qur'an tells a parable in this connection:

> 'The likeness of those who expend their wealth in the way of God is

as the likeness of a grain of corn that sprouts seven ears, in every ear a hundred grains. So God multiplies unto whom He will; God is All-embracing, All-knowing,' 2.261 (263); cf. Matthew 13.8.

The Qur'an urges people to give offerings before it is too late, before the day comes on which no trade, friend or intercession can help, 2.254 (255):

'Expend of what We have provided you before that death comes upon one of you and he says, "O my Lord, if only Thou wouldst defer me unto a near term, so that I may make freewill offering, and so I may become one of the righteous,"' 63.10.

It is obvious that the opposite of generosity, namely greed, is condemned by the Qur'an:

'You are called upon to expend in God's way, and some of you are niggardly. Whoso is niggardly is niggardly only to his own soul,' 47.38 (40).

'So fear God as far as you are able, and give ear, and obey, and expend well for yourselves. And whosoever is guarded against the avarice of his own soul, those – they are the prosperers,' 64.16.

Like the offering of *zakat* and the giving of contributions, the giving of gifts of love (*sadaqat*), a third expression which is used by the Qur'an in this connection, is also a characteristic of the believer, 70.24, 25, just as not giving is typical of the unbeliever, 75.31.

It is expressly said that giving in secret is preferable to giving openly:

'If you publish your freewill offerings, it is excellent; but if you conceal them, and give them to the poor, that is better for you, and will acquit you of your evil deeds; God is aware of the things you do,' 2.271.

'O believers, void not your freewill offerings with reproach and injury, as one who spends of his substance to show off to men,' 2.264 (266), cf. 4.38 (42).

It is also true that in *zakat* and the other contributions a reward is to be expected from God. God has prepared an unspeakable reward for submissive men and women who are believers, patient, humble, fasting, preserving their honour and giving gifts of love, 33.35:

'God blots out usury, but freewill offerings He augments with interest,' 2.276 (277).

'Surely those, the men and the women, who make freewill offerings and have lent to God a good loan, it shall be multiplied for them, and theirs shall be a generous wage,' 57.18 (17).

Therefore it is not surprising that the Qur'an urges the giving of gifts of love before it is too late; this is also said of the contributions, 63.10. As a definition of the gifts of love, the Qur'an says:

'The freewill offerings are for the poor and needy, those who work to collect them, those whose hearts are brought together (this refers to the newly converted), the ransoming of slaves, debtors, in God's way (i.e. the *jihad*, or holy war), and the traveller (literally "son of the way"); so God ordains; God is All-knowing, All-wise,' 9.60.

The position of the woman

What does the Qur'an say about the position of the woman and how she is to be treated? What are the rules for marriage and repudiation?

Two names of chapters in the Qur'an refer to this subject: chapter 4, which is called 'Women', and chapter 65, which is called 'Divorce'. In the Qur'an, at least in the framework of these regulations, the woman is almost exclusively discussed in relation to the man.

In matters of faith there is equality between man and woman:

'And whosoever does deeds of righteousness, be it male or female, believing – they shall enter Paradise, and not be wronged a single date-spot,' 4.124; cf. 40.40 (43); 16.97 (99) and 33.35.

The Qur'an does not allow marriage with women who are polytheists unless they come to believe, 2.221 (220). However, a marriage with a woman who belongs to the people of the book, Jews or Christians, is allowed for Muslims, 5.5 (7). Close blood relationships above all are mentioned as impediments to marriage, 4.22, 23 (26,27).

In marriage, intercourse with a woman during her period is not allowed, 2.222. But intercourse is allowed during the nights of Ramadan, the month of fasting – not, however, during the day, 2.187 (183). It is also forbidden during the pilgrimage, 2.197 (193).

The husband-wife relationship

How the relations between the husband and his wife are seen is evident from a text like this – in a particular connection, the Qur'an says that men stand one rank above women, 2.228:

'Your women are a tillage for you; so come unto your tillage as you wish, and forward for your souls; and fear God, and know that you shall meet Him. Give thou good tidings to the believers,' 2.223.

'Men are the managers of the affairs of women for that God has preferred in bounty one of them (men) over another (women), and for that they have expended of their property (a reference to the dowry). Righteous women are therefore obedient, guarding the secret for God's guarding. And those you fear may be rebellious admonish; banish them to their couches, and beat them. If they then obey you, look not for any way against them; God is All-high, All-great,' 4.34 (38).

The following text is constantly cited to justify polygamous marriage – the marriage of a man to a possible maximum of four wives at the same time. However, this text is connected with a regulation about orphans:

'If you fear that you will not act justly towards the orphans, marry such women as seem good to you (originally here the reference will have been to widows whose husbands perished in the battle of Uhud and were left with children for whom this text in fact wants to make a regulation), two, three, four; but if you fear you will not be equitable, then only one, or what your right hands own (the reference here is to slaves); so it is likelier you will not be partial,' 4.3.

Since the end of the nineteenth century the following verse from the same chapter is often quoted by Muslim exegetes; read in connection with the passage just cited it is meant to show that the Qur'an prescribes monogamy and not polygamy. At any rate according to the Qur'an one cannot practise justice when confronted with four wives at the same time:

'You will not be able to be equitable between your wives,' 4.129.

The witness of two women stands against that of one man, 2.282. As for questions of inheritance, the portion of one boy stands over against that of two girls, 2.282.

The behaviour of women

The Qur'an contains all kinds of rules about the behaviour and also the clothing of women, although men are also mentioned in this connection:

'Say to the believers, that they cast down their eyes and guard their private parts; that is purer for them. God is aware of the things they work. And say to the believing women, that they cast down their eyes and guard their private parts, and reveal not their adornment save such as is outward; and let them cast their veils over their bosoms, and not reveal their adornment save to their husbands or their fathers . . . or children who have not yet attained knowledge of women's private parts . . . And turn all together to God, O you believers; haply so you will prosper,' 24.31.

The rules about the clothing of older women is rather more flexible, 24.60 (59).

In the framework of the regulations about dealing with the Prophet and above all with his wives, the following clause appears:

'And when you ask his wives for any object, ask them from behind a *curtain*,' 33.53.

Here the word *hijab* is used, often translated veil. In fact this is something other than what is normally understood by veil.

In the case of immoral behaviour, four witnesses must be able to appear if an accusation is to be declared well-founded. If this is the case, those involved must be kept in their house until they can be killed or God indicates another way out, 4.15 (19). The regulation in this last text is regarded as abolished by another, which says that the adulterous wife and the adulterous husband each need to be scourged with one hundred strokes. If there is a false accusation, the false accusers will be stuck with eighty blows, 24.2–4. If the adultery is discovered by one of the relatives, then it is witnessed under oath and a curse is called down; it is then equal to the witness of four, 24.6,7.

Repudiation

According to the regulations of the Qur'an it is legitimate to repudiate a wife. If she proves to be pregnant within four months after that, the husband can take her back if he wishes, 2.226–228; cf. 65.1–7.

If the woman has been repudiated twice, then she may not remarry her first husband unless she first has married someone else and he has repudiated her in his turn, 2.229, 320. In all this the Qur'an calls on people not to transgress God's commandments, not to torment her and to treat her in a seemly way.

If the marriage with a woman is not yet consummated, then divorce or repudiation is possible on certain conditions, 2.236, 237 (237, 238); cf. 33.49 (48).

The Qur'an contains all kinds of regulations about the dowry if the woman is repudiated, 2.229, 236 (237), 237 (238); 33.49 (48).

Widows may marry again after observing a period of waiting of four months and ten days, 2.234, 235 (234–236).

Inheritance

The Qur'an also has a number of prescriptions about inheritance. Both men and women have a share of the estate of both parents and close relatives, 4.7 (8); here it is defined that relatives, orphans and the poor need to be maintained by them, 4.8 (9),

In a number of verses of the Qur'an more precise definitions are given about the extent of everyone's share, depending among other things on degrees of relationship, 4.11 (12), 12.12–16), 176 (175).

Punishments

The following can be said about the legislation relating to punishments in the Qur'an.

I have already mentioned how according to the Qur'an adulterers must be punished with one hundred strokes, 24.2 and how eighty strokes are the punishment for false witness, 24.4.

The thief must have his or her hand cut off:

> 'And the thief, male and female; cut off the hands of both, as a recompense for what they have earned, and a punishment exemplary from God; God is All-mighty, All-wise,' 5.38 (42).

As I have already said, where the death penalty for adultery is referred to, it is abolished by another text which prescribes flogging, 24.4.

The death penalty is to be inflicted on those who challenge God and His Messenger:

> 'This is the recompense of those who fight against God and His Messenger, and hasten about the earth, to do corruption there: they shall be slaughtered, or crucified, or their hands and feet shall alternately be struck off, or they shall be banished from the land. That is a degradation for them in this world; and in the world to come awaits them a mighty chastisement,' 5.33 (37).

This verse is preceded by a passage about Cain and Abel (not mentioned by name):

> 'Therefore We prescribed for the Children of Israel that whoso slays a soul not to retaliate for a soul slain, nor for corruption done in the land, shall be as if he had slain mankind altogether; and whoso gives life to a soul, shall be as if he had given life to mankind altogether,' 5.32 (35).

The Qur'an relates how the Pharaoh's magicians, who with their magic arts bear witness against those of Moses and Aaron, and to the scandal of Pharaoh come to believe, will have their hands cut off and be crucified, 7.124 (121); cf. 26.49 (48); 20.71 (74).

In another passage there is a mention of the death penalty:

> 'O believers, prescribed for you is retaliation, touching the slain; freeman for freeman, slave for slave, female for female. But if aught is pardoned a man by his brother, let the pursuing be honourable, and let the payment be with kindliness,' 2.178 (173).

The Qur'an also contains definitions of punishment and retribution in case of the killing of a believer:

> 'It belongs not to a believer to slay a believer, except it be by error. If any slays a believer by error, then let him set free a believing slave, and bloodwit is to be paid to his family unless they forgo it as a freewill offering,' 4.92 (94).

Passages to look up

Not all the prescriptions of the Qur'an are discussed here. Through the following references you can look up what the Qur'an has prescribed about these things:

The purification rituals before performing ritual prayer (*salat*): 4.43 (46); 5.6 (8,9).

The regulations about fasting in the month of Ramadan: 2.183–185 (179–181), 187 (183).

The regulations connected with pilgrimage: 2:196–200 (192–196); 203 (199); 2.158; 3. 97 (91).

The regulations about food, about what may or may not be eaten: 2.173 (168); 5.1,3 (4), 87, 88 (89, 90), 93 (94), 96 (97); 6.118–121, 141,
142 (142, 143), 145 (146); 16.114–116 (115, 117).

Regulations connected with wine: 5.90, 91 (92, 93); cf. 2.219 (216), 4.43 (46).

Regulations about the tribute that people of the book, Jews and Christians, must bring: 9.29.

Obligations with respect to the *jihad* ('holy war'): 2.190–195 (186–191), 216–218 (212–215); 3.167(160), 195 (194); 4.71–76 (73–78), 84 (86); 8.39 (40); 9.29, 36; 47.20 (22).

11

The Relationship with the People of the Book: Jews and the Story of Moses, Christians and the Story of Jesus

'He (Jesus) said, "Lo, I am God's servant; God has given me the Book and made me a Prophet. Blessed He has made me, wherever I may be; and He has enjoined me to pray, and to give the alms, so long as I live . . .

Peace be upon me, the day I was born, and the day I die, and the day I am raised up alive,"' 19.30, 31, 33, (31, 32, 34)

(On the minaret of Jam in Central Asia there is an inscription of the complete texts of this Mary chapter, from which some verses quoted above are taken.)

Introduction

By its own understanding, the message which Muhammad received, the Qur'an, stands in an explicit relationship to earlier books of revelation which were received before him. Thus there is mention of the scrolls' of Abraham, the Torah or 'scrolls' of Moses, the Psalms of David and the Gospel (the *injil*) of Jesus. Despite this connection, only rarely in the Qur'an is there what one could call a literal quotation from these books. But it does mean that Muhammad sees himself and his message as having a special relationship to the other 'people of the book', as they are called, especially to Jews and Christians. We shall look more closely at the relationship to them in general, both positive and negative, and then rather more specifically at the relations with Jews and Christians respectively; here the political context must not be ignored. The Jews and also the Christians are accused of having twisted their scriptures. That would also explain why they, or at least most of them, did not accept Muhammad's message and clearly deny the identity between this book of revelation and their own. A special place is occupied in the Qur'an by the story of Moses, which is even narrated at length on several occasions. The relationship with the Christians may above all initially have been better than that with the Jews, but as a result of political developments – the conflict with the Byzantine Christians – it deteriorated, above all in a later phase of Muhammad's ministry. The Qur'anic image of Jesus, fragmentary as it appears from the New Testament perspective, contains a number of key elements with points at which Christian views of Jesus are disputed.

Scrolls

In the discussion with Meccan opponents Muhammad is asked:

> 'They say, "Why does he not bring us a sign from his Lord? Has there not come to them the clear sign of what is in the former *scrolls*?"', 20.133; cf. 2.118 (112); 6.37.

This term can refer to the 'scrolls' of Abraham, 53.37 (38); 87.19 (but the Bible does not report that he brought something like a book). The Qur'an also speaks in the same connection of the 'scrolls' of Moses, 53.36 (37); 87.19.

The unbelievers ask for 'scrolls unrolled', 74.52.

The Qur'an which Muhammad brings is described as 'pages purified', 9.82. This revelation is written on 'pages high-honoured', 80.13. The thought is that the revelation with which Muhammad comes represents the heavenly archetype.

This becomes clear when we note how the term 'book' is used.

Book(s)

The expression 'book' or scripture occurs often in the Qur'an as a designation of the book of revelation:

> 'When there has come to them a Messenger from God confirming what was with them (books of revelation), a Party of them that were given the Book reject the Book of God behind their backs, as though they knew not (better),' 2.101 (95).

So this last means that some people of the book (Jews and Christians) were prepared to recognize the same message in the Qur'an, the revelation which came to Muhammad, and others were not, 2.121 (115).

In the Qur'an 'the book' can also denote the book of revelation that is given to Moses; cf. 2.44 (41), 53 (50), 85 (79); 6.91, 154 (155); 11.17 (20), 110 (112); 17.2,4; 2.49 (51); 32.23; 37.117; 40.53 (56):

> 'And We gave Moses the Book; and there was difference concerning it,' 41.45.

Torah (tawra)

Not only can the book of revelation to Moses be called 'book' or 'scrolls'; there is a more specific name for the book of Moses, namely Torah:

> 'Surely we sent down the Torah, wherein is guidance and light,' 5.44 (48).

It is said of the Jews that did not believe what Moses gave them in the Torah:

> 'But they, did they not disbelieve also in what Moses was given aforetime?,' 28.48.

> 'The likeness of those who have been loaded with the Torah, then they have not carried it, is as the likeness of an ass carrying books,' 62.5.

The Torah is communicated to Jesus, 5.110; Jesus is explicitly introduced speaking as someone who confirms the Torah that was before him, 61.6.

In line with this the Qur'an in turn confirms the scripture of Moses, and does so in Arabic:

> 'Yet before it was the Book of Moses for a model and a mercy; and this is a Book (the reference is to the Qur'an) confirming, in Arabic tongue, to warn the evildoers, and good tidings to the good-doers,' 46.12 (11).

But since according to the Torah there were Jews who did not believe in Moses, it is not so surprising that they do not want to believe in what Muhammad brings, 28.28.

The Psalms

'Psalms' is the designation for the book which according to the Torah is given to David.

> 'And We gave to David Psalms,' 17.55 (57); 163 (161); 38.29 (30).

The Gospel (injil)

The book of revelation that is given to Jesus is the Gospel, 5.110; 57.27 (26). While Jesus was already in the cradle the following words were put into his mouth:

> 'He said, "Lo I am God's servant; God has given me the book, and made me a Prophet,"' 19.30 (31).

So here the Gospel is called 'book':

> 'And We sent, following in their footsteps, Jesus son of Mary, confirming the Torah before him; and We gave to him the Gospel, wherein is guidance and light, and confirming the Torah before it, as a guidance and an admonition unto the godfearing,' 5.46 (50).

The Qur'an

The Qur'an is revealed to Muhammad, 6.19; he is inspired with it, 27.6. It says at the beginning of the Qur'an that there is no doubt in it and it is the right guidance for godfearers, 2.2. The Qur'an contains what earlier messengers proclaimed and confirms the scripture of Moses, 46.12.

> 'Naught is said to thee but what already was said to the Messengers before thee,' 41.43.

The specific characteristic of the Qur'an is that this confirmation is given in Arabic, 46.12 (11). The advantage of the Qur'an is that this can bring clarity and illumination. For example it explains to the Jews what they differ over:

> 'Surely this Qur'an relates to the children of Israel most of that concerning which they are at variance,' 27.76.

The Qur'an is the essential, 32.3 (2); the essential certainty, 69.51; it is sent down 'in truthfulness', 17.105 (106); there is no vanity, 41.42. The Qur'an is complete, 6.115; and contains decisive words, 86.13.

It is preserved on trustworthy tablets, 85.22; it is taken from the mother of scripture, who rests with God himself, 13.39; 43.4 (3); 3.7 (5). It is striking that the same thing is said of all books, especially the Torah, the Gospel and the Qur'an, namely that they give guidance and are a light; later prophets confirm former books, Jesus the Torah before him and Muhammad in his turn the Torah and the Gospel before him.

Quotations

Although there are also numerous places in the Qur'an which can be connected in one way or another with passages from the Bible, there are virtually no real quotations and literal borrowings. The following is an exception:

> 'For We (God) have written in the Psalms, after the Remembrance, "The earth shall be the inheritance of My righteous servant,"' 21.105.

Compare this passage with Psalm 37.13. This thought is also expressed in so many words in vv.9, 11, 22, and 34 of this psalm; cf. also Isaiah 60.21 and Matthew 5.5.

Thus another passage refers to the parable of the seed, 4.29, in which one can think of Matthew 13.8 or Mark 4.27. But the agreement there can be seen to be quite superficial and external.

Muhammad and the people of the book (Jews and Christians)
The relations of the prophet Muhammad to the Jews and Judaism can initially be described as positive. He followed them in various respects. Initially he prayed in the direction of Jerusalem, as Jews abroad used to do (see the example of Daniel, 6.11). He thought that in principle his message is the same as that revealed to Moses. His message was merely an Arabic version of that. Therefore it is obvious that Muhammad expected to find a willing ear among the Jews, indeed even acceptance and recognition. Moreover in some cases he got this:

> 'And some there are of the People of the Book who believe in God, and what has been sent down unto you (Muhammad), and what has been sent down unto them, men humble to God, not selling the signs of God for a small price,' 3.199 (198); cf. 5.66 (70).

The Qur'an also thinks that the Jew needs to be regarded as a kind of fellow believer:

> 'Dispute not with the People of the Book save in the fairer manner, except for those of them that do wrong; and say, "We believe in what has been sent down to us, and what has been sent down to you; our God and your God is One, and to Him we have surrendered,"' 29.46 (45).

The Qur'an even goes so far as to assert that the people of the book must be consulted in cases of doubt, 10.94. It is said of some of the people of the book that they are happy with what has been sent down to Muhammad, 13.36:

> 'And those to whom We have given the Book rejoice in what is sent down unto thee,' 13.36.

The following verse speaks very positively about the people of the book:

> 'Surely they that believe (i.e. the Muslims), and those of Jewry, and the Christians, and those Sabaeans, whoso believes in God and the Last Day, and works righteousness – their wage awaits them with their Lord, and no fear shall be on them, neither shall they sorrow,' 2.62 (59); cf. 5.69 (73); 22.17; 2.112 (106).

But the general attitude of the people of the book towards Muhammad is not positive. The Qur'an comes up against exclusivism, which characterizes particular Jews and Christians:

> 'And they say, "None shall enter Paradise except that they be Jews or

Christians." Such are their fancies. Say: "Produce your proof, if you speak truly,"' 2.110(105).

Clearly both want Muhammad and his people to become Jews or Christians:

> 'And they say, "Be Jews or Christians and you shall be guided,"' 2.135 (129).

> 'Never will the Jews be satisfied with thee (Muhammad), neither the Christians, not till thou followest their religion. Say: "God's guidance is the true guidance,"' 2.120 (114).

> 'Say the Jews and Christians, "We are the sons of God, and His beloved ones." Say: "Why then does He chastise you for your sins?",' 5.18 (21) (cf. Amos 3.2).

Over against some who accept Muhammad and the Qur'an stand others among the people of the book who according to the Qur'an keep the essential hidden, 3.17 (64) and mock religion, 5.57 (62). They are even accused of incitement to folly and unbelief, 2.109 (103); 3.69 (62), 72, 73 (65, 66), 99 (94), 100 (95): vengeance will be wrought on them because Muhammad has received the revelation, 5.59 (64); cf. 2.90 (84).

On the one hand a call is addressed to the people of the book, both Jews and Christians, to flock to Muhammad's side:

> 'Say: "People of the Book! Come now to a word common between us and you, that we serve none but God, and that we associate not aught with Him, and do not some of us take others as Lords, apart from God,"' 3.64 (57); cf. 5.65 (70).

On the other hand the Qur'an attacks the people of the book. One of the fiercest texts is certainly:

> 'Fight those who believe not in God and the Last Day and do not forbid what God and His Messenger have forbidden – such men as practise not the religion of truth, being of those who have been given the Book – until they pay the tribute out of hand and have been humbled,' 9.29; cf. also 9.30–35.

It is the conviction of the Qur'an that God himself will be the witness between Muhammad and the people of the book, 13.43. A decision will be made on the day of judgment:

> 'The Jews say, "The Christians stand not on anything"; the

Christians say, "The Jews stand not on anything"; yet they recite the Book.

So too the ignorant say the like of them. God shall decide between them on the Day of Resurrection touching their differences,' 2.113 (107).

Muhammad and the Jews

By 'Jews' the Qur'an understands those who confess or adhere to Judaism, 2.62 (59); 4.46 (48), 160 (158); 5.41 (45), 44 (48), 69; 6.146 (147); 16.118 (119); 22.17; 62.6.

The political context

The texts about the Jews that have been quoted must be understood against the background of the steadily deteriorating relations between Muhammad and the Jewish tribes in Medina. Whereas above all at the beginning, Muhammad conformed with all kinds of elements from Judaism and saw his message as connected with that of Moses, the more general positive response which was expected from the Jews of Medina failed to materialize

The texts which now follow reflect the ever-growing conflict from about the second year after the emigration (*hijra*) from Mecca to Medina. When Muhammad left for Medina in 622, he encountered not only two Arab tribes, but also three Jewish tribes. The Jews are also included in the treaty of Medina which was initially concluded: 'You your religion, I mine' is one of the stipulations of this treaty.

However, conflicts soon broke out. The Jews were accused secretly or openly of taking the side of Muhammad's opponents. Then first the Jewish tribe the Banu Qaynuqa' was banished from Medina, in April 624; later in August 625 the Jewish tribe, the Banu Nadir, whose palm trees were cut down, was banished, 59.2, 3, 15. The third Jewish tribe of the Banu Qurayza fare worst. Muhammad is afraid that they will betray him at the siege of Medina, 8,58 (6); 33.26. Six hundred male members of the tribe are killed!

'And He brought down those of the People of the Book who supported them (unbelievers) from their fortresses and cast terror in their hearts; some you slew, some you made captive,' 33.26.

The political and social situation does not excuse this attack on the Jews, but does partly explain it.

Positive attitude

It is known from the tradition that in Muhammad's time there were some Jews who became Muslims. There is also evidence of this in the

Qur'an, in so far as it is said that Jews who are believers recognize Muhammad as Prophet and they are sometimes called Muslim, 3.113 (109); 4.55 (58); 7.159.

> 'Those to whom We gave the Book before this believe in it (i.e. the Qur'an). And, when it is recited to them, they say, "We believe in it; surely it is the truth from our Lord. Indeed, even before it we had submitted,"' 28.52,53.

The Qur'an repeatedly calls on the Jews to believe:

> 'Children of Israel, remember My blessing wherewith I blessed you, and fulfil My covenant and I shall fulfil your covenant; and have awe of Me,' 2.40 (38).

> 'And believe in that I have sent down, confirming that which is with you, and be not the first to disbelieve in it. And sell not My signs for a little price; and fear you Me,' 2.41 (38); cf. 2.47 (44); 122 (116).

Negative attitude

But despite this appeal to the Jews to believe with a reference to the affinity between Muslims and Jews, the attitude of the majority towards Muhammad and his message is a negative one.

That is evident from the texts in the Qur'an, which become constantly more critical and fiercer. For example the Jews are depicted as those who think that later life is determined for them and not for others, 2.94 (88), although there are also some who are so attached to life that they want to live for a thousand years, 2.96 (90).

The Qur'an explains the specific food laws, especially the prohibitions on food, which did not apply previously, as a punishment on the Jews.

Jews are seen as unbelievers, 5.61 (66); as evildoers, 5.79 (82); as those who try to cause destruction, 5.64 (69); as enemies of the believers, 5.82 (85).

> '. . . you love them, and they love you not; you believe in the Book, all of it, and when they meet you they say, "We believe," but when they go privily, they bite at you their fingers, enraged. Say: "Die in your rage; God knows the thoughts in the breasts,"' 3.119 (115).

The Qur'an condemns those who take usury:

> 'And for their taking usury, that they were prohibited, and consuming the wealth of the people in vanity; and We have prepared for the unbelievers among them a painful chastisement,' 4.161 (159).

(Right from the very beginning the Qur'an opposes the desire of Muhammad's fellow citizens in Mecca to increase possessions excessively, 102.1).

Because of their belief, according to the Qur'an they are accursed, 2.88 (82); 4.46,(49), 52 (55); 5.13 (16), 60 (65), 64 (69), 78 (82).

Finally the prospect of punishment by fire is held out to them, 59.3.

The distortion of scripture (tahrif)

The Jews are accused of keeping part of scripture hidden, 2.174 (169). They conceal the revelation, 2.77 (72), or they twist or change God's words, 2.75–79 (70–73); 3.78 (72); 5.13 (16), 41 (45).

The accusation made by the Qur'an implies that they have plundered particular passages from the scripture which has been revealed to them:

> 'Are you (Muslims) then so eager that they (Jews) should believe you, seeing there is a party of them that heard God's word, and then tampered with it, and that after they had comprehended it, wittingly?,' 2.75 (70).

> 'So woe to those who write the Book with their hands, then say, "This is from God," that they may sell it for a little price; so woe to them for what their hands have written, and woe to them for their earnings,' 2.79 (73).

> 'Some of the Jews pervert words from their meanings, saying, "We have heard and we disobey,"' 4.46 (48).

As I said earlier, this question of distortion *(tahrif)* is looked at in different way. On the one hand a twisting of the meaning of scripture is read into it, and on the other a distortion or confusion of the text itself.

The nadir of relations is reached when dealings with Jews (and of course also with Christians) is forbidden, 3.118 (114); cf.5.51 (56) – where the Christians are also mentioned; cf. 58.14 (15). 'The people with whom God is angry' is often used as a designation for the Jews, 58.14 (15); cf. 1.6.

The children of Israel

When the Jews are mentioned in the Qur'an they are usually the contemporaries of Muhammad, the Jews of Medina, but when the term used is 'children of Israel', this is usually seen as a reference to the people of Moses, 2.54 (51), 60 (57), 67 (63); 5.20 (23); 7.128 (125), 148 (146), 159; 10.84; 14.6; 20.86 (88); 28.76; 61.5.

The children of Israel are indeed mentioned in connection with the Jews of Medina. These stories are often presented to explain their attitude and actions towards Muhammad. They do not want to believe in the revelation which has been sent down to Muhammad, despite the fact that – according to the Qur'an – this confirms what was revealed to them earlier. Then the Qur'an goes on to say:

> 'Say: "Why then were you slaying the Prophets of God in former time, if you were believers?,"' 2.90 (85); cf. also 3.181–184 (177–181).

What is said about the Israelites in the Qur'an is really primarily limited to the confrontation with Pharaoh in Egypt under the leadership of Moses and moments from the journey through the wilderness on the way to the Promised Land.

It is related how the people was oppressed by Pharaoh, 7.127 (124); Pharaoh made them his slaves, 26.22 (21):

> 'Now Pharaoh had exalted himself in the land and had divided its inhabitants into sects, abasing one party of them, slaughtering their sons, and sparing their women; for he was of the workers of corruption,' 28.4 (3).

God wanted to deliver or free the children of Israel:

> 'Yet We desired to be gracious to those that were abased in the land, and to make them leaders, and to make them the inheritors, and to establish them in the land, and to show Pharaoh and Haman, and their hosts, what they were dreading from them,' 28.5, 6 (4, 5).

Moses asked Pharaoh to let him lead his people out:

> '. . . so send forth with me the children of Israel', 7.105 (103), 143 (131); 20.47 (49); 26.17 (16).

Moses took upon himself the leadership of the children of Israel, 10.83–87.

The children of Israel were led over the sea, 7.138 (14); 20.77:

> 'And we brought the children of Israel over the sea; and Pharaoh and his hosts followed them insolently and impetuously till, when the drowning overtook him, he said, "I believe that there is no god but He in whom the children of Israel believe; I am of those that submit,"' 10.90.

The Israelites are saved and delivered from the tyranny of Pharaoh,

7.141 (137); 20.80 (82); 44.30 (29) and inherit the dwellings and treasures of Pharaoh 26.59; 44.28 (27).

The children of Israel wanted to worship idols, 7.138–140 (134–136). On Mount Tur or Sinai God summoned a meeting, 20.80 (82). The mountain was raised up above them, 2.63 (60), 93 (87); 4.154 (153). (According to a Jewish legend, when the Israelites did not want to accept the law which was given to Moses, God made Mount Sinai tower above their heads in order to terrify them.)

God made a covenant with the children of Israel:

> 'Children of Israel, remember My blessing wherewith I blessed you, and fulfil My covenant and I shall fulfil your covenant; and have awe of Me,' 2.40 (38); cf. 2.80 (74), 83 (77), 93 (87); 5.12, 15, 70 (74).

Scripture was given to the children of Israel, 45.16 (15), which has been made right guidance for them, 17.2; 32.23; 40.53 (56). They are called God's elect:

> 'Children of Israel, remember My blessing wherewith I blessed you, and that I have preferred you above all beings,' 2.47 (44); cf. 2.122 (116), 40 (38).

They were also given the prophets, 45.16 (15):

> 'And We bequeathed upon the people that were abased all the east and the west of the land (in other words the whole land) We had blessed; and perfectly was fulfilled the most fair word of the Lord upon the Children of Israel, for that they endured patiently,' 7.137 (133).

However, they turned away from the covenant, 2.83 (77), 100 (94) and thought it of little worth, 3.187 (184); they violated the covenant, 4.155 (154); 5.13 (16).

They made a calf as an idol, 2.51 (48), 92 (86), 93 (87); 7.148–152 (146–151); 20.88, 89 (90, 91).

They did not want to enter the holy land, 5.21–25 (24–28) and then they had to wander around for forty years in the wilderness, 5.2–29. Disunity arose among them after knowledge had come to them, 10.83, and they began to differ over scripture, 11.110 (112); 41.45.

According to the Qur'an the children of Israel have killed messengers and prophets with no justification, 2.61 (58), 91 (85); 3.112 (108), 181 (177); 183 (180).

> 'So, for their breaking the compact, and disbelieving in the signs of God, and slaying the Prophets without right, and for their saying,

"Our hearts are uncircumcised" – nay, but God sealed them for their unbelief, so they believe not, except a few,' 4.155 (154).

> 'And We took compact with the Children of Israel, and We sent Messengers to them. Whensoever there came to them a Messenger with that their souls had not desire for, some they cried lies to, and some they slew,' 5.70 (74).

Jesus is also a messenger of whom the Qur'an says that he was sent to the children of Israel, 3.49 (43) and served as an example for them, 43.59.

One group believed in him, another did not, 61.6.

Finally the assertion is refuted that they killed and crucified Jesus, as the Jews claim according to the Qur'an, 4.157 (156).

Moses' early life

One of the most extended narratives about a prophet in the Qur'an concerns the figure of Moses; he is a prophet and messenger, 19.51 (52); a prophet with whom God has made a covenant, 33.7. The Qur'an tells how as a child Moses was thrown in the river in a chest and then rescued and brought up at the court of Pharaoh, 20.37–41; 26.18; 28.7–13; here mention is made both of his mother, 20.38, 40; 28.7 (6), 10 (9); 13 (12) and of his sister, 20.40 (48); 28.11 (10), 12 (11).

> 'Said Pharaoh's wife, "He will be a comfort to me and thee. Slay him not; perchance he will profit us, or we will take him for a son." And they were not aware,' 28.9 (8).

We are told how in a quarrel between an Egyptian and an Israelite Moses comes between them and commits murder, 20.40 (41); 26.14 (13), 19 (18); 28.15 (14), 33. He then flees from Egypt, 28.21 (20), and spends some time in Midian, 20.40 (42); 28.22–26; there he marries one of the daughters of that people, 28.27, 28.

The call of Moses

Moses is called by God in the valley of Tuwa, 19.52 (53); 27.7–12; 28.29–35; 79.15,16:

> 'Hast thou received the story of Moses? When he saw a fire, and said to his family, "Tarry you here; I observe a fire. Perhaps I shall bring you a brand from it, or I shall find at the fire guidance." When he came to it, a voice cried, "Moses, I am thy Lord; put off thy shoes; thou art in the holy valley, Tuwa. I Myself have chosen thee; therefore give thou ear to this revelation. Verily I am God; there is no god

but I; therefore serve Me, and perform the prayer (*salat*) of My remembrance. The Hour is coming; I would conceal it that every soul may be recompensed for its labours. Let none bar thee from it, that believes not in it but follows after his own caprice, or thou wilt perish."

"What is that, Moses, thou hast in thy right hand?"

"Why, it is my staff," said Moses. "I lean upon it, and with it I beat down leaves to feed my sheep; other uses also I find in it." Said He, "Cast it down, Moses!" and he cast it down, and behold it was a serpent sliding. Said He, "Take it, and fear not; We will restore it to its first state. Now clasp thy hand to thy arm-pit; it shall come forth white, without evil. That is a second sign. So We would show thee some of Our greatest signs,"' 20.9–23 (cf. Exodus 2.1–7).

Moses and Pharaoh

Moses is sent to Pharaoh on behalf of his people, 25.36 (38). He asks him to let the children of Israel go, 26.17(16); cf. 26.10–15 (9–14), 16–33 (15–32); here he also performs signs, 27.12; 28.32; 29.39 (38); 43.46–48 (45–47); 79.20; 40.26.

The Qur'an goes on to relate that Moses is sent to Pharaoh with nine proofs, 17.101 (103); cf. 11.96 (99). The Qur'an presumably arrives at this number by counting the transformation of the staff into a snake and the making of the hand white (leprosy) as two of these proofs. The other seven are the 'plagues' of Egypt: the famine, flood, locusts, lice, frogs, blood and last the 'plague', presumably the killing of the first-born, cf. 7.130–135 (127–131) (Exodus 8.4–11; 24–28; 9.27–35; 10.16–20.)

In different places the Qur'an mentions the duel between Moses and Pharaoh's magicians, in which Moses gets the opportunity to perform miracles, 7.103–126 (101–123); 10.75–82 (76–82); 20.37–76 (59–78); 26.34–51 (33–51).

Moses is regarded by Pharaoh, Haman and Korah as a lying magician, 40.24 (25); 43.49 (48) and is thought contemptible by Pharaoh, 43.52 (51):

'And Pharaoh said, "Let me slay Moses, and let him call to his Lord. I fear that he may change your religion, or that he may cause corruption to appear in the land." And Moses said, "I take refuge in my Lord and your Lord from every man who is proud, and believes not in the Day of Reckoning."

Then said a certain man, a believer of Pharaoh's folk that kept hidden his belief, "What, will you slay a man because he says, 'My Lord is God,' yet he has brought you the clear signs from your Lord?

> If he is a liar, his lying is upon his own head; but if he is truthful, somewhat of that he promises you will smite you. Surely God guides not him who is prodigal and a liar,"' 40.26–28 (27–29).

The passage through the sea
God saves his people from terrible straits, 37.115. At God's command Moses leads the people through the sea:

> 'Also We revealed unto Moses, "Go with My servants by night; strike for them a dry path in the sea, fearing not overtaking, neither afraid,"' 20.77 (79, 80); 26.52; 44.23, 24 (22, 23).

In fact Moses divides the sea with his staff, 26.63.

> 'Pharaoh followed them with his hosts, but they were overwhelmed by the sea,' 20.78 (81).

In this way the people is saved, 2.50 (47); 7.138 (134); 26.65.

Revelation on Sinai
The meeting between Moses and God takes place on Mount Tur (Sinai):

> 'And when Moses came to Our appointed time and his Lord spoke with him, he (Moses) said, "Oh my Lord, show me, that I may behold Thee! (cf. Exodus 33.20)." Said He, "Thou shalt not see Me; but behold the mountain – if it stays fast in its place, then thou shalt see Me." And when his Lord revealed Him to the mountain He made it crumble to dust; and Moses fell down swooning. So when he awoke, he said, "Glory be to Thee! I repent to Thee; I am the first of the believers,"' 7.143 (139, 140).

Moses receives the tables of the law:

> 'And We wrote for him on the Tablets of everything an admonition, and a distinguishing of everything: "So take it forcefully, and command thy people to take the fairest of it. I shall show you the habitation of the ungodly,"' 7.145 (142).

When Moses comes down the mountain he discovers the idolatry which has developed in the meantime. During his absence for forty days on Mount Sinai a golden calf has been made, 7.138–140 (134–136); 2.51 (48); 5.148 (146,147). Moses accuses his people of worshipping the calves, 2.51–55; 7.149–153 (148–152); 20.86–94

(88–95). He breaks the tables of the law, 7.150 (149). The children of Israel ask Moses to show them God, 2.55 (52). Of the other events on the journey through the wilderness the Qur'an also mentions that when water is needed Moses strikes the rock with his staff, 2.60 (57); 7.160 (cf. Numbers 20).

Moses rebukes the people for being discontented with certain food, 2.61 (58) (cf. Numbers 11.4ff.).

Moses commands his people to enter the holy land, but they are afraid of the violent people there. However, there are two who fear God and trust in victory. But the people's entry into the land is blocked for forty years, 5.20–26 (23–29).

One of the special passages about Moses which has no parallel in the Bible can be found in 18.65–83 (64–81). This is about a companion of Moses whose name is not mentioned and who tests his patience. In Islamic tradition this figure is called al-Khidr, 'the green man'.

The specific position of Moses

The special position occupied in the Qur'an by Moses, who was greatly respected by God, 33.69, is connected with the fact that God spoke to him directly, 4.164 (162); 7.143 (139). This is an intimate conversation of someone entrusting secrets to another.

> '. . . We brought him near in communion,' 19.52 (53).

That means that Moses is shown a special favour:

> 'And those Messengers, some We have preferred above others; some there are to whom God spoke, and some He raised in rank,' 2.253 (254).

Later Moses is called *kalim Allah* to express the special favour that *God spoke to him*.

Christians

In certain passages in the Qur'an Christians and Jews are linked with the Muslims:

> 'Surely they that believe, and those of Jewry, and the Sabaeans, and those Christians, whosoever believes in God and the Last Day, and works righteousness – no fear shall be on them, neither shall they sorrow,' 5.69 (73); cf. 2.62 (59).

God will pass his judgment at the last judgment:

> 'Surely they that believe, and those of Jewry, the Sabaeans, the

> Christians, the Magians and the idolaters – God shall distinguish between them on the Day of Resurrection; assuredly God is witness over everything,' 22.17.

Christians are described in the Qur'an as those who are closest to Muslims:

> 'Thou wilt surely find the most hostile of men to the believers are the Jews and the idolaters; and thou wilt surely find the nearest of them in love to the believers are those who say "We are Christians"; that, because some of them are priests and monks, and they wax not proud,' 5.82 (85).

The Qur'an follows this with a description of Christians who clearly believe Muhammad's message:

> '. . . and when they hear what has been sent down to the Messenger, thou seest their eyes overflow with tears because of the truth they recognize. They say, "Our Lord, we believe; so do Thou write us down among the witnesses,"' 5.83 (86).

The Qur'an says that God has made a covenant with Christians, but that they have forgotten part of what they have been admonished to do. God causes division and enmity among them, 5.14 (17). There is also division between Jews and Christians, 21.93; 23.53 (55); 43.65.

The Qur'an speaks appreciatively of priests and monks and says that they are not proud, 5.82 (85):

> 'And We set in the hearts of those who followed him (Jesus) tenderness and mercy. And monasticism they invented – We did not prescribe it for them – only seeking the good pleasure of God,' 57.27.

Likewise, according to the Qur'an the Christians will not be content until Muhammad follows their teaching, 2.131 (129).

It is doubtless because of the political circumstances – the defeat which the Muslims suffer in Mu'ra in September 629 against the Byzantine Christians, 48.16 – that the preaching about the Christians takes on a sharper tone. Christians are then often attacked in the same breath as the Jews:

> 'If thou (Muhammad) followest their (the Jews' and Christians') caprices, after the knowledge that has come to thee, thou shalt have against God neither protector nor helper,' 2.120 (114); cf. 2.135 (129).

For example, the Qur'an finds fault with the Christians for their own views, for having called their monks and the Messiah their Lord alongside God., 9.31. The Qur'an sees Christians as being entangled in lies, because they say that the Messiah is God's son, 9.30.

In a particular situation the Qur'an forbids taking Christians as allies, 5.51 (56); cf. 6.1,9; 3.28 (27), 118 (114); 4.89 (91); 9.23.

There is a call for an attack on Jews and Christians.

The Qur'anic picture of Jesus

By comparison with the biblical material, the portrait of Jesus in the Qur'an, like that of Moses and the other prophets, can be said to be fragmentary. The passages about Jesus appear above all, though not exclusively, in two chapters, from the Meccan (19) and the Medinan periods (3).

Precisely because the picture is so fragmentary, it is striking that the history of the annunciation and birth of Jesus, which is limited in the New Testament (only in the Gospels in Luke's account and briefly in the Gospel of Matthew), appears in the Qur'an twice, in chapters 19 and 3.

The birth of Jesus is announced to Mary, 19.16–21; 3.42–46 (37–41). He is given her as a son by God breathing spirit into her, 21.91.

The Qur'an describes the birth, 19.22–26 (22–27). Both Jesus and his mother are made a sign, 23.50 (52); cf. 21.91.

The Qur'an relates the miracle that in the cradle Jesus speaks as an adult in order to refute insults directed at his mother – getting a child without anyone touching her, 3.46 (41), 5.110 (109):

> 'Mary pointed to the child (Jesus as a child in the cradle) then; but they said, "How shall we speak to one who is still in the cradle, a little child?" He (Jesus) said, "Lo, I am God's servant; God has given me the Book, and made me a Prophet. Blessed He has made me, wherever I may be; and He has enjoined me to pray (*salat*), and to give the alms (*zakat*), so long as I live, and likewise to cherish my mother; He has not made me arrogant, unprosperous. Peace be upon me, the day I was born, and the day I die, and the day I am raised up alive!",' 19.28–33 (30–34).

It is also said of Jesus that he performs miracles. He creates birds out of clay and breaths life into them – with God's consent. He heals the blind and lepers and brings the dead to life, always with God's consent. Jesus asks God – at the request of his disciples – to make a table come down from heaven, 5.112–119. The apostles are called helpers of Jesus, 3.52 (45); 61.14.

God has given Jesus instructions in scripture, wisdom, Torah and the Gospel, 5.110; 3.48 (43).

Jesus is mentioned after Noah, Abraham and Moses as a prophet with whom God has made a covenant, 33.7. In the Qur'an he is also called the messenger to the children of Israel; this was confirmed before him in the Torah. He also predicts the coming of a messenger after him. This text is interpreted by Muslims as a prediction by Jesus of the coming of Muhammad:

> 'And when Jesus son of Mary said, "Children of Israel, I am indeed the Messenger of God to you, confirming the Torah that is before me, and giving good tidings of a Messenger who shall come after me, whose name shall be Ahmad . . .,"' 61.6.

In the Qur'an Jesus is not always called God's messenger but also 'His word' and 'His spirit', 4.171 (169). Proofs are given him and he is strengthened with the spirit of holiness, 2.87 (81); 2.253 (254); 5.110 (109).

The Gospel is given to Jesus, 57.27.

The Qur'an makes a comparison between Adam and Jesus in the way in which he is created:

> 'Truly, the likeness of Jesus, in God's sight, is as Adam's likeness; He created him of dust, then said He unto him, "Be," and he was,' 3.59 (52).

It is said of Jesus that he is highly respected in this and in later life, and he is put close to God, 3.45 (40).

As well as being often called 'Isa, the son of Mary, Jesus is often called messiah in the Qur'an, 3.45 (40), 171 (169), 172 (170).

Jesus is called a model for the children of Israel, 43.59. The Qur'an says that God protects Jesus for the children of Israel, 5.110. He is the one who shows the children of Israel what foods are permitted, 3.49 (43). The Qur'an says that those of the children of Israel who are unbelievers are cursed by Jesus, 5.78 (82).

To the Christians, the Qur'an emphasizes that Jesus was only a servant of God:

> 'The Messiah will not disdain to be a servant of God,' 4.172 (170); 43.59.

In the Qur'an Jesus explicitly denies that he is a god or God:

> 'And when God said, "O Jesus son of Mary, didst thou say unto men, 'Take me and my mother as gods, apart from God'?" He said, "To Thee be glory! It is not mine to say what I have no right to. If I indeed said it, Thou knowest it, knowing what is within my soul, and I

know not what is within Thy soul; Thou knowest the things unseen,"' 5.116.

(It can be seen from this verse that the Qur'an regards the Trinity as consisting of God, Jesus and Mary!) In this way the Qur'an wants to refute the fact that Christians make Jesus Lord or declare that the Messiah is the Son of God, 9.30. The Qur'an calls such a conviction clear unbelief, 5.17 (19), 72 (76).

The aim of the judgment to which Muhammad calls the Christians – this is the Christian delegation from Najran which once visited him – is to force a solution to this question:

'And whoso disputes with thee (Muhammad) concerning him (Jesus), after the knowledge that has come to thee, say: "Come now, let us call our sons and your sons, our wives and your wives, our selves and your selves, then let us humbly pray and so lay God's curse upon the ones who lie,"' 3.61 (54).

One of the most important texts in the Qur'an relating to the controversy over Jesus between Christians and Muslims is, however, one which stands in the context of a dispute with the Jews. The Jews are accused of having broken their covenant, of not believing in God's signs, of having killed the prophets and having insulted Mary. The Qur'an then goes on:

'. . . and for their (the Jews) saying, "We slew the Messiah, Jesus son of Mary, the Messenger of God" – yet they did not slay him, neither crucified him, only a likeness of that was shown to them. Those who are at variance concerning him surely are in doubt regarding him; they have no knowledge of him, except the following of surmise; and they slew him not of a certainty – no indeed; God raised him up to Him; God is All-mighty, All-wise. There is not one of the People of the Book but will assuredly believe in him before his death, and on the Resurrection Day he will be a witness against them,' 4.157–159 (156–157); cf. 3.55 (48), 43.61.

Passages to look up

For the relationship between the Qur'an and the Bible make the following comparisons: 7.40 (38) with Matthew 19.24.

For 2. 178 (173) cf. Leviticus 24.17–21.

For 3.181–184 (177–181) cf. I Kings 18; Leviticus 9.24.

For 5.45 (29) cf. Exodus 21.23–25; Leviticus 24.19f.; Deuteronomy 10.21.

For 7. 143 (139) cf. Exodus 33.18–25.

For 7.195 (194) cf. Psalm 115.5ff.

For 7.40 (38) cf. Matthew 19.24; Mark 10.25; Luke 18.25.

However, some stories about Jesus and Moses can be read side by side as they appear in the context of the Qur'an.

For Moses: 20.9–98; 28.3–42.

For Jesus: 3.33–63; 19,.16–36 (16–37).

12

Christians and the Qur'an

'Moses heard once heard a shepherd praying:
"O God, show me where you sit
that I may become your servant.
I want to clean your shoes,
comb your hair,
make your clothes,
and bring milk for you."

When Moses heard him pray in such a foolish way he rebuked him with the words:

"You fool, have you become an unbeliever? God is spirit and has no need of these services which you offer him in your ignorance."

The shepherd was so ashamed by this rebuke that he rent his garments and fled into the wilderness.

At that moment a voice was heard from heaven saying,

"O Moses, why have you sent away my servant? It is your task to reconcile a man with me and not to drive him away from me."'

(A story from the tradition of the Islamic mystics)

Introduction

This chapter is about more than just getting to know the Qur'an.

For centuries there has been barren polemic between Christians and Muslims, but here a new attempt is being made to talk about the significance of Jesus Christ in particular in the light of the Qur'an, which seems to deny particular Christian ideas about Jesus.

Does it make sense for a Christian to read the Qur'an?

It is understandable that reading the Qur'an raises all kinds of questions for Christians. An unprejudiced reader will doubtless get the impression that much knowledge of the Old and New Testaments is recognizable. However fragmentary the stories about biblical figures may be in the Qur'an, they do sound familiar and seem known. All kinds of passages about trust in God and different prayers are related to the Psalms and the prayer traditions of Jews and Christians.

From both the Jewish and the Christian side scholars have investigated what the Qur'an may have taken from Judaism and Christianity.

An orthodox Muslim will generally regard such an investigation as illegitimate, because he often sees it as an attack on the authority and originality of the Qur'an. Muslims see the Qur'an as the word of God that Muhammad has received directly through revelation without the intermediary of Jews or Christians. Therefore any notion of borrowing is rejected.

However, there are also Muslims who think rather differently here. Also on the basis of the Qur'an, which clearly reports the relationship between the Qur'an, the Torah and the Gospel, they think that such an investigation and a comparison with earlier books may be engaged in and does also make sense.

Fazlur Rahman, a Pakistani scholar, has written that in his view the Qur'an is entirely the word of God and entirely the word of Muhammad. He has not been thanked for this statement. For this reason all kinds of actions were taken against him in Pakistan at the time. Certainly such an approach to the Qur'an is quite close to a Christian understanding of the Bible. Christians too can call the Bible on the one hand the Word of God and at the same time the words of its human authors, for example the prophet Isaiah or the evangelist Luke.

Of course it makes sense to read the Qur'an because of the Muslims who also live in many Western countries. For them the Qur'an is a holy book, from which they want to live and which they see as the Word of God for their lives. But is there also a deeper reason why Christians should read it?

Some Christians will not think it necessary for them and their fellow believers to reflect on the content of the Qur'an. They interpret the saying of the apostle Paul, 'For I decided to know nothing among you except Jesus Christ and him crucified' (I Corinthians 2.2), to mean that Christians need not know anything about Muhammad and the Qur'an (or any other holy book).

But there is much in favour of Christians and Muslims taking each others' books seriously. That does not mean that either of them should water down or relativize each other's writings. The Qur'an itself gives Muslims reason to enter into conversation with the people of the book, both Jews and Christians:

> 'So, if thou art in doubt regarding what We have sent down to thee, ask those who recite the Book before thee,' 10.94.

> 'Dispute not with the People of the Book save in the fairer manner,' 29.45.

From the Christian side the conversation with the Muslims about the Qur'an can be approached in the conviction that God has not left himself without witness (Acts 14.17) and that traces of God's concern can be discovered in the appearance of Muhammad and in the Qur'an.

Christians could ask themselves whether God does have something to say through Muhammad and the Qur'an which Christians could reflect on with profit. That something of the kind is possible is beginning to be realized as a result of encounters between Jews and Christians.

However, if we look back on the centuries-old relations between Christians and Muslims, there is not much stimulus for talking about dialogue. The two communities have fought each other in holy war and crusade. For centuries there has been polemic. Or for centuries there has been silence. Christian minorities in the Islamic world were often glad to be left in peace; Muslims for their part usually do not feel the need to talk about their faith with Christians in any depth.

But if one argues for an approach and mutual dialogue, this is done in the conviction that for all kinds of reasons such a mutual encounter really makes sense: Christians and Muslims are each other's fellow human beings and at least in many Western countries are fellow-countrymen and women: they both believe in God who has created human beings, who has sent His prophets and made His desires known, that His creatures may live on this earth according to His commandments.

But do not all kinds of problems arise, particularly when one reflects on the specific content of the conversation? Is not the Qur'an a book which shows a great affinity with Judaism and Christianity but which also opposes Jewish and Christian ideas of faith? Jesus may be known, but has the significance which Christians have attached to him in the past and attach to him in the present been recognized?

It is obvious that on many points which could and must be worked out in more detail, Christians are particularly interested in what the Qur'an says about Jesus. There was also lengthy discussion of them in the past – at least when there could be said to have been an encounter. The arguments which were used time and again were usually unconvincing to the other party. Often arguments on both sides have been and are stereotypes. It is clear that it makes little sense to continue the conversation in such a way.

Here I shall try to approach in a different way the understanding of Jesus Christ, which at least for Christians is the most important point. I shall try to indicate how it is possible for Christians to take seriously what is said about Jesus Christ in the Qur'an. A comment by Ali Merad can be seen as an encouragement from the Muslim side to undertake such an investigation: he argues that some statements about Jesus in the Qur'an are made as certainties, whereas others are proposed as a subject for further reflection with Christians.

The discussion between Christians and Muslims on the meaning of Jesus Christ focusses on two points. First comes the question whether Jesus is the Son of God or God, and connected with that whether he is one of the Three (in One). The second issue is the crucifixion of Jesus, which seems to be denied by the Qur'an. We shall go more closely into these two points, on the understanding that by no means everything can be said within the limits of this chapter. In a sense more questions will be raised than answers given.

Jesus and God

The Qur'an accuses Christians of having made Jesus a second God. The Qur'an has Jesus himself dispute this notion:

> 'And when God said, "O Jesus son of Mary, didst thou say unto men, 'Take me and my mother as Gods, apart from God'?", He said, "To Thee be glory! It is not mine to say what I have no right to. If I indeed said it, Thou knowest it, knowing what is within my soul, and I know not what is within Thy soul; Thou knowest the things unseen,"' 5.116.

We get the impression from this text that the Qur'an regards the doctrine of the Trinity as relating to God, Jesus and Mary. Elsewhere the Qur'an again emphatically denies that Jesus is one of the three, 4.171 (169). Here one could rightly ask whether what the Qur'an denies is what Christians generally believe. At any rate the church has always rejected belief in three gods as heresy.

Clearly in his day Muhammad must have met Christians whose faith came close to believing in two or three gods. When I once said in the presence of Muslims that this was a misunderstanding, a Muslim emphatically denied that it was. At that time he referred to his experiences in Spain where he felt that people talked in such a way about God the Father and Mary (the mother) and the child, that – at least there – there was tritheism in his experience. Be this as it may, Christians must ask whether they have always confessed and still confess their own faith and religion sufficiently carefully. Could it not be that Christians sometimes speak in such a way of Jesus that the impression can easily be given that he is part of a kind of binity, for example when they talk of the Old Testament God of punishment and the New Testament God of love? Do they not often lose sight of the fact that God was in Christ reconciling the world to himself (II Corinthians 5.19)?

The Qur'an denies that Jesus is the Son of God because that would imply that God had children and intercourse with a woman. For this reason the Qur'an also never calls God 'Father'. From the beginning of Muhammad's activity it is denied that God has children, sons or daughters. In short, it amounts to the fact that God can have no children because he can have no wife. This idea is rejected by the statement:

> 'who has not begotten, and has not been begotten,' 112.3.

Now Christians will argue that when they use this title 'son' in talking about Jesus they are not thinking of a physical father-son relationship. And Christians will join with Muslims in rejecting the notion of polytheism. Then the question mentioned above again arises, namely whether the Qur'an really denies what Christians believe. Many Muslims would continue to answer yes to this question. In other words, they would continue to regard the doctrine of the Trinity as belief in three gods, or polytheism. And they will continue to regard the titles used of Jesus in the New Testament like 'Son of God' as so many indications of the stubborn way in which Christians hold to polytheistic images.

However, if Christians and Muslims are ready to keep listening to each other, an attempt can be made to indicate that Christian faith is not about the divinization of a human being.

Here a story may help to bring some clarification.

Once a group of Chinese and a group of Greeks came to the court of the emperor of China. Each group thought that it was better than the other. The emperor decided to put the two groups with their conflicting claims to the test. Each group was assigned one of two adjoining rooms. Both were called on to create a work of art. The Chinese set to work and made a painting on one of the walls. The Greeks in the adjoining room polished their wall so smooth that it began to shine like a mirror. As soon as the Chinese had finished, they invited the emperor to marvel at their work of art. The emperor went quiet when he saw the beauty of the painting. After that he went to the Greeks in the next room, who thereupon removed the curtain which hung between the two rooms, whereupon the splendid picture of the Chinese artists was reflected in their wall polished like a mirror, and thus looked even more beautiful than it was.

The 'moral' of the story is that the human heart is like such a mirror. The human heart must be cleansed and purified from sin so that the image of God can be reflected in it.

This comparison between the heart and a mirror appears both in the Christian and in the Islamic mystical tradition. It indicates that human beings must so cleanse their hearts that they can reflect God's likeness. 'God has become man that man may become God,' said the church father Irenaeus.

In this connection the Eastern Orthodox speak of *theosis*, divinization. Does this word mean that human beings are ontologically divinized? The image of the mirror makes it clear that this is not the case.

Once when I was lecturing in Indonesia to a group of Muslim students I was asked about the meaning of the crucifixion of Jesus. I first asked a question in return, 'Was Al-Hallaj justly executed?' (Al-Hallaj was a great Islamic mystic in Iraq who claimed 'I am God', *ana'l*

Haqq. For this reason he was crucified in Baghdad in 922.) One of the students answered by saying, 'Al-Hallaj's mistake was that he said this publicly.'

The Gospel of John describes how Jesus is accused of blasphemy: 'The Jews answered him: We stone you for no good work but for blasphemy; because you, being a man, make yourself God' (John 10.33). There are Jews who could give a similar answer about Jesus to the one that this Muslim gave about Al-Hallaj, namely that he should not have made the messianic secret public. In the Gospel of Mark it is striking how much Jesus urges that the fact that he is Messiah should be kept secret.

This is not to suggest that the issue is precisely the same with Al-Hallaj and Jesus, with Jews, Muslims and Christians. Nor is the intention to put Al-Hallaj and Jesus on the same footing. Nor would the image of the mystical union with God in the story of the mirror quoted above fully explain the mystery of Jesus' special and unique relationship to the one whom he called 'Father' (*Abba*). But these considerations could perhaps help us to speak with more awe and reverence about the mystery of Jesus Christ and his relationship to God.

When the Qur'an says elsewhere that Jesus did not think it beneath his dignity to be a servant of God, 4.172 (170), cf. 43.59, is it saying any more than what the 'song of the Son of man' from Paul's letter to the Philippians says, namely that he did not shrink from taking the form of a slave (Philippians 2.7)? The Qur'anic term 'servant' (*'abd*) is close to the Hebrew *'ebed*. Can we perhaps hear in these texts something of a criticism of what is sometimes too triumphalistic talk of Jesus as Lord? Not that Christians should want to deny this confession. Otherwise they would no longer be Christians. This confession stands in the very same hymn about the Son of man, 'Jesus Christ is Lord' (Philippians 2.11). But have not Christians perhaps forgotten that this is about the servant *('abd, 'ed),* who is confessed as Lord? Have they not also often forgotten that this hymn ends with 'to the glory of God the Father' (Philippians 2.11)? Does not the apostle Paul also say elsewhere that when everything is subject to him, the Son will also subject everything to him who has subjected all things to him, that God may be all in all (I Corinthians 15.2)?

Do not these biblical passages all warn against all tendencies to worship two or three gods which sometimes are or have been present among Christians? Can Christians perhaps learn again in encounters with Jews and Muslims how powerfully and resolutely the Bible teaches the unity of God? Cannot the encounter lead to a deeper understanding of the Old and New Testaments?

This is not to sweep away the differences. Those between Jews, Christians and Muslims remain.

The differences continue in the first instance to concern the person of Jesus. Christians have from the beginning believed that Jesus, who did his work as servant/slave of his Father – as the obedient son – was bound in a unique way to God as his Father (*Abba*) (the 'like God' with which the song of the Son of man begins, Philippians 2.6).

But provided that Christians and Muslims do so with respect and openness towards one another, they can ask each other about each other's holy scripture. Challenged by the witness of the Muslims, Christians can then try to give an account of their Christian faith.

The crucifixion of Jesus

The second crucial subject between Christians and Muslims centres on the question of the crucifixion of Jesus. For most Muslims it is clear that the Qur'an denies that Jesus was crucified. Some will think that it is not very meaningful to ask about the nature of this denial by the Qur'an. It could be seen by Muslims as an attempt to give a Christian twist to the exegesis of the Qur'an, an exegesis which can be understood as something that is suggested because it suits the Christians.

Despite these understandable hesitations about such an undertaking, it does make sense to go into this question. In my view this arises from wanting to take one another seriously.

The core of the Christian message can be summed up as Jesus crucified and risen. Over against that the Muslims say: Jesus not crucified and risen (or elevated to God).

Is not this denial, at least as most Muslims have constantly understood the Qur'an, an insuperable stumbling block? Can this barrier ever be removed. The classic Qur'an text says:

> '. . . and for their saying, "We slew the Messiah, Jesus son of Mary, the messenger of God" – yet they did not slay him, neither crucified him, only a likeness of that was shown to them. Those who are at variance concerning him surely are in doubt regarding him; they have no knowledge of him, except the following of surmise; and they slew him not of a certainty – no indeed; God raised him up to Him; God is All-mighty, All-wise. There is not one of the People of the Book but will assuredly believe in him before his death, and on the Resurrection Day he will be a witness against them,"' 4.157–159 (156–157).

Christian readers of the Qur'an have time and again been struck that other passages in the Qur'an speak quite plainly of Jesus' death:

> 'Peace be upon me, the day I was born, and the day I die, and the day I am raised up alive!' 19.33 (34).

And elsewhere:

> 'I will take thee to Me and will raise thee to Me, and I will purify thee of those who believe not,' 3.55 (48).

The term that is translated here as 'take thee to Me' means the return to God for the last judgment. This return is the work of God, the angels or the angel of death (or death). In the Qur'an it is twice used of Jesus.

So it seems that on the one hand the Qur'an says that Jesus died and on the other hand that God raised him. The usual Muslim view is that he is exalted without dying. In that case the testimony of the Qur'an on this point is indeed diametrically opposed to the Christian witness. But the Qur'an seems to speak not only of the exaltation of Jesus but at the same time of his death.

Now the view could be defended that in the famous text 4.157–159 (156–57), the Qur'an is not so much denying the Jesus was killed, but above all wants to deny that human beings (in this case the Jews) were responsible for his death. The Qur'an says that it was not the Jews but God himself who required it, 3.55 (48).

Such an exposition could be defended with a reference to the Qur'an itself. At Badr a small group of Muslim supporters of Muhammad won a decisive battle against their Meccan opponents. As once in the case of Gideon (cf. Judges 7), a small group can win the victory over a great host of enemies. The Qur'an then says:

> 'You did not slay them, but God slew them,' 8.17.

Now one can say of this Qur'an passage that it is clear that the Muslims did indeed defeat the Meccans. They killed a number of their opponents. But clearly this text wants to say that it was God who gave them the victory. He killed them. If scripture can explain scripture, then that could also be the interpretation of this cryptic text, 4.157–59 (156–57).

A Muslim who had given a great deal of thought to the meaning of Jesus Christ according to both the Bible and the Qur'an asked of these apparently conflicting Qur'an verses: could it not be that the different expressions – God made him die; He exalted him to Himself; and this third text where the crucifixion seems to be denied – are about one and the same event? Cannot the same event be being described under different aspects?

Is it the case, it could be asked, that the New Testament describes one and the same event from different aspects?

The Risen Lord asks the two disciples on the way to Emmaus, 'Was it not necessary that the Christ should suffer these things in order to enter into his glory?' (Luke 24.26). Now this text could be read as if it were about two events, of which the second followed the first exclusively chronologically: suffering and resurrection. But cannot it also be read in such a way that the two aspects are very closely connected? In the Gospel of John it is said that Jesus was 'exalted on the cross'. And as Moses raised up the snake in the wilderness, so the Son of man must be raised (John 3.14). John does not separate this raising up, this elevation on the cross, from the exaltation to heaven. The first is more the presupposition of the last.

If the Qur'an could be interpreted as indicated above, do not the Qur'an and the New Testament perhaps stand less far apart on this point than is often supposed by both Christians and Muslims?

Conclusion

It is clear that many Christians and Muslims at best do not think such an interpretation of the Qur'an and the Bible relevant. On the whole the present situation is characterized by a revival of fanaticism. In particular we can think of the renaissance of a fundamentalist Islam. But fundamentalism is not a phenomenon that one encounters only on the Muslim side. Deep feelings of self-satisfaction can be perceived on both sides. Many Muslims think that they do not need Christians, just as many Christians think that they do not need Muslims. On both sides people think that they know all that they need to know or all that is commanded in matters of faith; often they also think that they know what others know or could know. Particularly when that is indeed the prevailing meaning and conviction, there is little use in an attempt at exposition as given here.

But if one believes that people need other people, and also that Muslims need Christians and Christians Muslims, it makes a lot of sense to get into and remain in conversation with one another in order to arrive at a clear picture of each other's faith and one's own faith, at a deeper understanding of what the Bible and the Qur'an have to say about how God wants to speak to us today. Christians need not fear such an encounter or think it a denial of their scripture.

Both Christians and Muslims have to learn to get rid of any form of self-sufficiency and self-satisfaction. Unless they do that, like Moses in the story quoted at the beginning of this chapter, they can be found guilty of driving away from God people who truly believe in him.

Appendixes

1. Index of persons, subjects and place names in the Qur'an
This list gives in alphabetical order the names of persons and places which occur in the Qur'an or to which allusions are made. One or more significant passages are always mentioned.

Aaron	Harun, 20.30–33 (29–32)
Abel	The name itself does not appear in the Qur'an, 5.30(33); in the Muslim tradition the name is Habil
Abolition	Of one Qur'an text by another, 2.106 (100); 16.101 (103)
Abraham	Ibrahim, 2.124–141 (118–135)
Abu Bakr	The first caliph or successor of Muhammad; not mentioned by name, 9.30
Abu Lahab	This is an uncle of Muhammad, a fiery opponent to the end, 111.1
'Ad	The people of 'Ad received a message from Hud, 7.65ff. (63ff.)
Adam	2.30–37 (28–34)
'Adn	See Eden. The garden of Eden, as a designation for Paradise
'Ahmad	Is regarded as a reference to Muhammad, 61.6.
Alexander the Great	He is not mentioned by name, 18.83ff. (Dhu.l-Qarnayn)
Al-Lat	A goddess, 53.19
Alliance	20.115 (114); 2.83 (77); 93 (87)
Alms	*zakat* (opposite of usury), 2.276 (277)
Alyasa'	See Elisha
Amram	Imram, 3,33–35 (30–131) (also called the father of Mary)
Andrew	Idris, 21.85; 19.56, 57 (57, 58).

Angel	7.206 (205); 21.19,20. See also Gabriel, Harut and Marut
Antioch	Not mentioned by name, 36.13 (12).
Apostasy	This means apostasy from Islam, 5.54 (59); 16,106, 108
Aus	One of the Arab tribes in Medina
Ayesha	Muhammad's wife, not mentioned by name, 24.11–26.
Ayyub	See Job
Azar	The father of Abraham, 6.74
Babylon	Babil, 2.102
Badr	Battle of Badr, 2.123 (119)
Bedouins (Arabians)	49.14–18
Belief	4.136 (135)
Believer	2.285
Benjamin	Not mentioned by name, 12.63–66
Book	People of the book (Jews and Christians), 2.105 (99), 109 (103)
Byzantines (Greeks)	Rum, 30.2
Cain	Not mentioned by name, 5.30 (33); called Kabil in the Islamic tradition
Calf	Worship of the calf by the Israelites, 2.51 (48), 92 (86)
Cave	The people of the cave (the seven sleepers of Ephesus), 18.9–26 (8–25)
Creation	2.117 (111); 7.54 (52)
Crucifixion	Of Jesus, 4.157 (156)
David	Dawud, 38.21–26 (20–25)
Dawud	See David
Devil	See Iblis
Dhu l-Qarnayn	See Alexander the Great
Eden	'Adn, 6.72 (73)
Egypt	Misr, 2.61 (58)
Elders	17.23, 24 (24, 25)
Elijah	Ilyas, 37.123
Elisha	Alyasa, 6.123
Emigrant	Those who left Mecca with Muhammad for Medina, 4.100 (101)

Enoch — See Idris
Eve — Not mentioned by name, 2.35 (33)
Ezra — 'Uzayr, 9.30

Fasting — 2.183–185 (179–181)
Fir'aun — See Pharaoh
Forgiveness — 22.38–43 (36–41)

Gabriel — Jibril, 2.97, 98 (91, 92)
Gog and Magog — Jajuj and Majuj, 18.94 (93)
Goliath — Jalut, 2.251 (252)
Gospel — 3.56 (58)
Greeks — See Byzantines
Guidance — 2.12 (114)

Hafsa — One of Muhammad's wives, daughter of his friend 'Uman, not mentioned by name, 66.4
Haj — See Pilgrimage
Haman — 28.6 (5)
Harun — See Aaron
Harut — An angel, sent with Marut to judge the earth, 2.102 (96)
Hell — 38.55–58
Helpers — Of Muhammad in Medina, 9.100 (101)
Hijr — Name of a city which no longer exists in the north of the Hejaz (the area where Mecca and Medina lie), 15.80–84
Hud — An Arab prophet, 7.65–72 (63–70)
Hunayn — A city between Mecca and Tai'f, scene of a battle shortly after the conquest of Mecca, 9.25
Hypocrites — 4.61 (64)

Iblis — The devil, 7.11–18 (10–17); see also Satan
Ibrahim — See Abraham
Idolatry — *shirk*, 4.48 (51)
Idris — See Andrew, sometimes thought of as Enoch
Ilyas — See Elijah
Imran — See Amram
Inheritance — 4.11–14 (12–19)
Injil — See Gospel
Intercession — 2.48 (45)

'Isa	See Jesus
Isaac	Ishaq, 2.133
Ishaq	See Isaac
Islam	As the name of the religion, 3.19 (17); as submission to God, 9.74 (75).
Ishmael	Isma'il, 2.125 (119) ff.
Isra'	See Night Journey
Israel	Isra'il, 19.58 (59)
Isra'il	See Israel
Jacob	Jaqub, 2.132, 133, 136 (126, 127, 130)
Jajuj and Majuj	Gog and Magog
Jalut	See Goliath
Jerusalem	Not mentioned. Probably alluded to in 17.48–51 (43–44)
Jesus	'Isa, 19.27–36 (28–37)
Jews	2.111 (105)
Jibril	See Gabriel
Jihad	See (Holy) War (literally: 'effort on God's way')
Job	Ayyub, 4.163
John	Yahya, 3.38–41 (33–36)
Jonah	37.139–148
Joseph	Jusuf, all of 12
Judgment	Day of judgment, 20.105–108 (105–107)
Junus	See Jonah
Jusuf	Joseph
Ka'ba	2, 125–127 (119–121)
Khaybar	Jewish oasis, expedition to this place, 48.15.
Khazraj	One of the Arab tribes in Medina
Khidr	Unknown companion of Moses, 18.65–82 (64–81). He plays an important role in the Muslim mystical tradition
Korah	Qarun, 28.76–82 (possibly the story is also connected with that of Croesus)
(Al-)Lat	A goddess, 53.19
Light verse	24.35
Lokman	31.12–19 (11–18), a hero from pagan Arabia who is granted a long life
Lot	Lut, 11.77–83 (79–84)
Lut	See Lot

Madyan	See Midian
Magi	Zoroastrians
Majus	Zoroastrians, see Magi
Man	22.5
Manat	Goddess, 53.20
Marib Dam	34.16 (15)
Marriage	2.221 (220)
Marut	An angel, 2.102 (96), see Harut
Mary	Miriam, 19.16ff.
Mary, the Coptic	66.3
Masih	See Messiah
Mecca	48.24
Medina	9.101
Messengers	9.163–165 (161–163)
Messiah	3.45 (40)
Michael	Mika'il, 2.98 (92), an archangel alongside Gabriel
Midian	Madyan, 7.85–93 (83–91)
Mika'il	See Michael
Misr	See Egypt
Monk	5.82 (85)
Moses	Musa, 20.36–40 (36–41)
Muhammad	3.144 (138)
Musa	See Moses
Night journey	Isra', 17.1
Nimrod	2.258 (260) is said to be an allusion to him
Nineveh	not named, 10.98
Noah	Nuh, 7.59–64 (57–62)
Nuh	See Noah
Paradise	3.133–136 (127–130)
People of the Book	Jews and/or Christians, 2.105 (109)
Pharaoh	Fir'aun, 28.3–42 (2–42)
Pilgrimage	Haj, 2.196–200 (192–196)
Potiphar	Neither he nor his wife are mentioned by name
Prayer	As ritual prayer (*salat*), 73.20; as 'free prayer' (*du'a*), 3.38 (33)
Prophets	2.213 (209)
Psalms	Zabur, 4, 163 (161)
Qarun	See Korah

Qur'an	12.1
Quraysh	Tribe in Mecca, 106.1
Ramadan	2.185 (181)
Repentance	4.16–18 (20–22); 25.70,71
Resurrection	27.67
Retribution	2.178,179 (173–175)
Rum	See Byzantines
Saba'	Sheba
Sabaeans	2.62 (59)
Salat	see Prayer
Salih	An Arab prophet sent to Thamud, 7.73–79 (71–77)
Samaritan	Samarit. These are said to have made the golden calf. In the Qur'an this explains the break between the Israelites and the Samaritans, 20.85–96 (87–96)
Samarit	See Samaritan
Samuel	Not mentioned by name, 2.246 (247)
Sarah	Not mentioned by name, 3.40 (35); 51.29
Satan	12.5; see Iblis
Saul	Talut, 2.247–249 (248–250)
Sheba	Saba'. 27.22–44 (22–45)
Shirk	See Idolatry
Sinai	Sina, see Tur
Sju'ayb	This Arab prophet is sent to Midian, 7.85–93 (83–91)
Sodom and Gomorrah	Not mentioned but alluded to, 15.61–77; 7.80–84 (78–82); 9.70 (71); 53.53,54 (54.55); 69.9
Solomon	Sulayman, 27.15–45
Sulayman	See Solomon
Tabuk	An expedition to Tabuk, not mentioned by name, 9.38–52
Talut	See Saul
Tawrah	See Torah
Thamud	This is the tribe to which Salih is sent, 7.73–79 (71–77)
Torah	Tawrah, 3.50 (44)
Tur	Sinai, 52.1; 19.52 (53)
Trench	Battle round Medina, in 627, 33.9–21.
Uhud	3.102–179 (97–174)

Unbelievers	2.6, 7 (5, 6)
Usury	2.274–281 (276–281)
‘Uzayr	See Ezra
Uzza	A goddess, 53.19
War	2.218 (215)
Washings	For ritual prayer, 5.6 (8,9)
Wine	2.219 (216)
Women	4.127–130 (126–129)
Yathrib	Old name for Medina, 33.13
Zabur	See Psalms
Zakariya	See Zechariah
Zakat	See Alms
Zechariah	Zakariya, 3.37 (32)
Zayd	Muhammad’s adopted son, not mentioned by name, 33.37
Zaynab	Wife of Zayd and after the divorce wife of Muhammad, not mentioned by name, 33.37
Zoroastrians	See Magi

2. *Data from the life and ministry of Muhammad*

This appendix mentions some of the most important moments and events in the life of Muhammad and his community. Where possible references are given to the Qur’an. Here the chronological order is followed.

570	In the chapter ‘the elephant’ 105 there is a reference to an expedition by the Abyssinian ruler Abraha of Yemen, who advanced against Mecca in 570. This planned attack came to a premature end because – according to the most natural explanation – an epidemic of plague broke out in his camp. According to tradition Muhammad was born in that precise year. Muhammad is born the son of ‘Abdallah, who died before his birth, and Amina, who died when he was about six years old. There is an allusion to this event in 93.6.
c.578	His grandfather ‘Abd al-Muttalib (578) takes care of Muhammad. After his death, his uncle, Abu Talib, the father of ‘Ali, looks after him.
c.595	Muhammad becomes ‘rich’ through his mar-

	riage to the rich merchant's widow Khadijah, 93.9.
c. 610	His first appearance as a prophet is around 610, 74.
c. 615	The first emigration (*hijra)* takes place. It consists of a number of followers of Muhammad (89 men and 18 women are mentioned) because of the pressure they have to endure in Mecca.
c. 616	The conversion of 'Umar.
616–618	During this period Muhammad's family is boycotted by his opponents.
619	The year of the death of his uncle Abu Talib and his wife Khadiyah.
*c.*620	Around this time Muhammad makes a vain attempt to win over the tribe of Thaqif in Ta'if, a neighbouring city, to his cause. Only *jinns* are said to have listened to his message.
622	On his flight from Mecca to Medina Muhammad spends some time with his friend Abu Bakr in a cave to escape his pursuers, 9.40.
	The emigration (*hijra*) in 622 of Muhammad with around 70 of his followers from Mecca to Medina is later chosen as the beginning of the Islamic reckoning of time.
623	At the end of this year the treaty of Medina is concluded; it includes the Jews.
624	In January the attack on the Meccan caravan at Nakhla takes place, 2.216, 217 (212–214).
	The break with the Jews comes about in January/February.
	The battle of Badr takes place in March; it is one of the first important victories that Muhammad and his followers win over their Meccan opponents, 8.5–12; 41–44 (42–46); 3.123 (119).
	In April the Jewish tribe of the Banu Qaynuqa' (which is allied with the Arab tribe of Khazraj) is the first to be banished from Medina, 59.2,15. For the hardening of the attitude towards the Jews see 2.88,89 (82,83).
625	The victory of the battle of Uhud, which is less successful for the Muslims, takes place in March, 3.121–128 (117–123), 138–175 (132–169).

	In August the Jewish tribe of the Banu Nadir is besieged, their date palms are cut down and they are driven to the oasis of Khaybar, 59.5,8.
626	In the spring Muhammad contracts a marriage with Zaynab, the divorced wife of his adopted son Zayd, 33.37.
626/627	In December 626/January 627 an expedition is undertaken against the Banu -l Mustaliq, 45.14 (13); 63.8.
627	In April the battle in the trenches takes place in defence of Medina, which has been besieged by the Meccans, 33.9–21.
	The liquidation of at least the bulk of the male members of the Jewish tribe of Banu Qurayza follows this event, 33.26; 8.56 (58).
628	The expedition to Hudaybiyya takes place in March. In this month Muhammad makes a treaty with his Meccan opponents at this place, at the frontier of the consecrated territory. It is resolved not to make the pilgrimage to Mecca originally planned, but to hold it the next year, 48.18–21.
	In May a military campaign is carried out against the Jews in Khaybar, around 100 miles to the north of Medina, 48.15, 19, 27.
629	In March the pilgrimage to Mecca takes place on the basis of the treaty of Hudaybiyya,
	In September the Muslims suffer a defeat from the Byzantines near Mu'ta south of the Dead Sea, 48.16.
630	The conquest (*fath*) of Mecca takes place in January, 9.17,18.
	The same month sees the battle with Hunayn, 9.25,26. In February the city of Ta'if is besieged. The division of the booty from Hunayn takes place in February/March.
630/631	Between April 630 and April 631 Muhammad receives various delegations.
630	In October/November the campaign against Tabuk takes place; the location is mentioned in the Qur'an without a name, 9.38–52,118 (119).
631	Muhammad receives a Christian delegation from Najran, 59–63 (52–56).

	In March Muhammad has a proclamation read out during the pilgrimage, 9.3–28.
632	In February/March the farewell pilgimrage takes place, 2,196 (192); 5.52.
	Muhammad dies on 8 June 632.

3. Bibliography

A. J. Arberry, *The Qur'an Interpreted*, London 1955

D. Bakker, *Man in the Qur'an*, Amsterdam 1965

W. Beltz, *Die Mythen des Koran. Der Schlüssel zum Islam*, Berlin and Weimar 1980

K. Cragg, *The Event of the Qur'an. Islam in its Scriptures*, London 1971

—, *The Mind of the Qur'an*, London 1973

T. Izutsu, *God and Man in the Koran; Semantics of the Koranic Weltanschauung*, Tokyo 1964

—, *Ethico-religious Concepts in the Qur'an*, Montreal 1966

J. Jomier, *The Great Themes of the Qur'an*, London 1997

Seyyed Hossein Nasr, *Ideals and Realities*, London 1966

R. Paret, *Der Koran. Kommentar und Konkordanz,* Stuttgart, Berlin, Cologne and Mainz 1971

D. Rahbar, *God of Justice*, Leiden 1960

F. Rahman, *Major Themes of the Qur'an*, Minneapolis 1980

—, *Islam* , London 1966

N. Robinson, *Discovering the Qur'an. A Contemporary Approach to a Veiled Text*, London 1990

C. C. Torrey, *The Commercial-Theological Terms in the Koran*, Leiden 1892

K. Wagtendonk, *Fasting in the Qur'an*, Leiden 1968

W. M. Watt, *Companion to the Qur'an*, London 1967

—, *Bell's Introduction to the Qur'an*, Edinburgh 1970

Select Index